Cambridge Elements ≡

Elements in Publishing and Book Culture
edited by
Samantha Rayner
University College London
Leah Tether
University of Bristol

THE TRADE IN RARE BOOKS AND MANUSCRIPTS BETWEEN BRITAIN AND AMERICA *C.* 1890–1929

Danielle Magnusson

University of London

Laura Cleaver

University of London

CAMBRIDGE
UNIVERSITY PRESS

CAMBRIDGE
UNIVERSITY PRESS

Shaftesbury Road, Cambridge CB2 8EA, United Kingdom

One Liberty Plaza, 20th Floor, New York, NY 10006, USA

477 Williamstown Road, Port Melbourne, VIC 3207, Australia

314–321, 3rd Floor, Plot 3, Splendor Forum, Jasola District Centre,
New Delhi – 110025, India

103 Penang Road, #05–06/07, Visioncrest Commercial, Singapore 238467

Cambridge University Press is part of Cambridge University Press & Assessment,
a department of the University of Cambridge.

We share the University's mission to contribute to society through the pursuit of
education, learning and research at the highest international levels of excellence.

www.cambridge.org
Information on this title: www.cambridge.org/9781009069052

DOI: 10.1017/9781009070102

First published 2022

A catalogue record for this publication is available from the British Library.

ISBN 978-1-009-06905-2 Paperback
ISSN 2514-8524 (online)
ISSN 2514-8516 (print)

Additional resources for this publication at www.cambridge.org/rarebooks_resources

The Trade in Rare Books and Manuscripts between Britain and America *c.* 1890–1929

Elements in Publishing and Book Culture

DOI: 10.1017/9781009070102

First published online: August 2022

Danielle Magnusson
University of London

Laura Cleaver
University of London

Author for correspondence: Danielle Magnusson, danielle.magnusson@sas.ac.uk

ABSTRACT: This Element examines the trade in rare books and manuscripts between Britain and America during a period known as the 'Golden Age' of collecting. Through analysis of contemporary press reports, personal correspondence, trade publications, and sales records, this study contrasts American and British perspectives as rare books passed through the commercial market. The aim is to compare the rhetoric and reality of the book trade in order to assess its impact on emerging cultural institutions, contemporary scholarship, and shifting notions of national identity. By analysing how markets emerged, dealers functioned, and buyers navigated the market, this Element interrogates accepted narratives about the ways in which major rare book and manuscript collections were formed and how they were valued by contemporaries.

KEYWORDS: collecting history, book history, manuscript studies, library history, cultural history

ISBNs: 9781009069052 (PB), 9781009070102 (OC)
ISSNs: 2514-8524 (online), 2514-8516 (print)

Contents

     The following are available online at
     www.cambridge.org/rarebooks_resources:

Introduction

In October 1889, *The Book Lover*, a monthly journal published by the New York bookseller William Evarts Benjamin, addressed the transatlantic book trade. It declared:

No book importer can shut his eyes to the fact that the English book dealers and the American book buyers are yearly getting closer together. The English rare book dealer has the advantage over his American competitor in having the best market at hand to supply demand and less expense of conducting business. The American dealer has the client at hand, an apparent advantage which is largely discounted by the glamour which attracts the collector who proudly boasts he 'gets his books direct from London'.[1]

Although a more famous American bookseller, Dr Abraham Rosenbach, later traced the origins of American book collecting to *c.* 1840, the period from *c.* 1890 to the Wall Street Crash in October 1929 can be seen as its 'Golden Age'.[2] This era included the creation of collections by J. Pierpont Morgan (which on his death in 1913 passed to his son J. Pierpont Morgan Jr), Henry Folger, Henry Huntington, and Henry Walters, all of which became part of museums and libraries that bear their founders' names. In addition, Americans who are now less well-known created libraries that included rare books and manuscripts. The formation of these collections was facilitated by transatlantic networks of buyers, sellers, and dealers. Moreover, the decisions made by all those involved in the trade not only shaped cultural institutions but informed scholarship on rare books and notions of national and cultural identity. At auctions those with less disposable wealth, whether public libraries or private collectors, could only acquire what was not bought by the wealthiest. In addition, some rich collectors sponsored scholarship about items in their collections,

---

[1] [untitled article], *The Book Lover*, 1(9), October 1889, p. 1.
[2] A. S. W. Rosenbach, 'Why America Buys England's Books', *The Atlantic Monthly*, October 1927, p. 452.

enhancing the status and potential economic value of books, and consequently of themselves and their libraries. The relationship between America and Britain was presented in the contemporary press as particularly significant for the international book market. American demand and British supply created a successful trade. In contemporary sources the term English was often used synonymously with British. Yet although united by a common language and shared history, the import and export of rare books exposed tensions in both Britain and America around ideas of shifting economic and cultural power and the value of the past for the present.

In 1889 it was not obvious that a 'Golden Age' of American book collecting was nascent. At the end of that year, news reached America that the renowned London-based (Prussian-born) bookseller Bernard Quaritch was to send his son, Bernard Alfred (known as Alfred to distinguish him from his father) to America with an exhibition of what Quaritch called 'a peerless collection of books and manuscripts' for sale to the bibliophiles of America.[3] The response from American dealers was hostile. An article in *The New York Times* concluded that 'the general opinion among booksellers here is that Quaritch has brought nothing to this country which he could sell in England', and *The Collector* urged Americans to buy at American sales.[4] At the same time, one dealer was quoted as saying 'there are more American book buyers who are ignorant of what they buy than those who have a knowledge of books', observing that 'if the Quaritch sales should be successful there might be a boom in this peculiar trade. Whether it will be successful or not is a question'.[5]

Alfred Quaritch arrived in New York in January 1890 and set out his stock at the Albemarle Hotel in Madison Square.[6] Among his early customers were

---

[3] B. Quaritch, *Exhibition of Books & MSS by Bernard Quaritch of London* (London: Bernard Quaritch, 1890).

[4] 'Quaritch's "Rare Books": Some Sharp Opinions from New-York Dealers', *NYT*, 26 January 1890, p. 14; 'Milking the Cow', *The Collector*, no. 5, January 1890, p. 39.

[5] 'Quaritch's "Rare Books"', p. 14.

[6] See also L. A. Morris, 'Bernard Alfred Quaritch in America', *The Book Collector*, special number for the 150th Anniversary of Bernard Quaritch (1997), 118–33; R. A. Linenthal, '"The Collectors are Far More Particular Than You Think:" Selling Manuscripts to America', *Manuscripta*, 51(1) (2007), pp. 131–42.

people who had previously bought books from the Quaritch firm, demonstrating that there were already collectors in the United States. These included Brayton Ives, William Augustus White, and Marshall Lefferts.[7] In New York Alfred met other collectors, notably the printing press manufacturer Robert Hoe as well as Norton Quincy Pope and his wife Abbie.[8] In 1884 Hoe and Ives had been among the founding members of the Grolier Club in New York (named after the sixteenth-century French collector Jean Grolier de Servières), which brought together a community of those interested in rare books. Yet recognising that wealth was not confined to the East coast, Alfred ventured beyond the New York community of bibliophiles, visiting Boston, Chicago, Cincinnati, Pittsburgh, and Philadelphia in search of new clients.

Although generally disappointed by his lack of sales, Alfred's trip was partially redeemed by Theodore Irwin of Oswego's purchase of the Golden Gospels (described in Quaritch's catalogue as an eighth-century manuscript on purple vellum) with only a small discount from the asking price of $12,500/£2,500.[9] In addition to manuscripts, which were written by hand and therefore unique items, Quaritch took rare printed books to America. These included a Psalter printed by Fust and Schoeffer in 1459, marketed by Quaritch as 'The second book printed with a date; the second book from the press of Fust and Schoeffer; the costliest book ever sold, as well as one of the most beautiful' and priced at $26,250.[10] The early printed books also

[7] London, Bernard Quaritch Ltd., letters from B. A. Quaritch to B. Quaritch, 27 January 1890 and 29 January 1890; see also Rosenbach, 'Why America Buys', p. 455; C. L. Cannon, *American Book Collectors and Collecting from Colonial Times to the Present* (New York: H. W. Wilson, 1941), pp. 152–4, 147–50, 329–31; D. C. Dickinson, *Dictionary of American Book Collectors* (New York: Greenwood Press, 1986), pp. 179–80, 199, 335–6.

[8] London, Bernard Quaritch Ltd., letters from B. A. Quaritch to B. Quaritch, 5 February 1890 and 19 February 1890; C. Ryskamp, 'Abbie Pope, Portrait of a Bibliophile', *The Book Collector*, 33(1) (1984), pp. 39–53; M. E. Korey and R. Mortimer, 'Fifteen Women Book Collectors', *Gazette of the Grolier Club*, 42 (1990), pp. 86–8; Morris, 'Quaritch in America', p. 188.

[9] See Morris, 'Quaritch in America', pp. 194–5; the manuscript is now New York, Morgan Library, M.23.

[10] Quaritch, *Exhibition of Books*, p. 6.

included one produced by Johannes Gutenberg, whose Bible would become one of the most sought-after books of the twentieth century, and works by the first English printer; William Caxton. Books printed before 1500, known as incunabula, survive in relatively small numbers, making them particularly appealing to collectors. Quaritch's other offerings included illustrated books, bindings, English literature, and Americana. Of the 457 catalogued items, 289 were dated to before 1600 (most of the rest being Americana), and material of this era (rendered rare because limited material survives from that period) will be the focus of this Element.

In 1902 the Grolier Club published *One Hundred Books Famous in English Literature*, of which fourteen had been printed before 1600. Such publications provided potential shopping lists for unimaginative collectors. Two of the works could have been bought from Quaritch's 1890 exhibition: John Gower's *Confessio Amantis* published in 1483 (offered by Quaritch for $1,250), and William Langland's *Piers Ploughman* published in 1550 ($52.50, with four leaves wanting), while further titles could have been obtained in different editions. The perceived need for the Grolier Club's list suggests a growing interest in the rarities of English literature, but also collectors' need for guidance, a role often filled by dealers like Quaritch. However, even in 1890, Alfred found his American visitors unexpectedly demanding, carefully inspecting the books and asking questions.[11] This echoed a story in *The Book Lover* which quoted an 'English rare book dealer' as having declared: 'Our English collectors don't pretend to be so careful and painstaking'.[12] Yet in 1890 Bernard Quaritch sought to reassure a despondent Alfred, urging him to 'Persevere, my dear boy, you are sowing now seed for future harvests', a prediction which was to prove accurate.[13] For example, although Alfred only sold two medieval manuscripts whilst in America, at least a further nine of the manuscripts in the exhibition later returned to the United States.[14]

[11] London, Bernard Quaritch Ltd., letter from B. A. Quaritch to B. Quaritch, 27 February 1890; Linenthal, 'The Collectors', p. 135.
[12] [untitled article], *The Book Lover*, 1(9), October 1889, p. 1.
[13] Oxford, Bodleian Library, MS Eng. Lett. c. 435, f. 106.
[14] These manuscripts in America are now: Los Angeles, J. Paul Getty Museum, MS Ludwig IX.20; New Haven, Beinecke Library, MS 402; New York, Columbia

Although Alfred Quaritch was underwhelmed by America in 1890, the rare book trade between Britain and the United States grew exponentially over the next four decades. By the end of the century the Quaritch firm received regular commissions from America. Bernard Quaritch died in 1899, leaving the business to his son, and from 1901 Alfred made annual trips across the Atlantic, until taken ill in New York in 1911.[15] The rare book trade was part of a broader investment in libraries and cultural institutions for America. In 1901 *The Chicago Tribune* reported another record year for philanthropy, with $15,388,732 given to libraries, much of it by Andrew Carnegie (who also sponsored libraries in Britain).[16] In this era the American rare book market was driven by a few extremely rich individuals including Hoe, Morgan, Huntington, and Folger, supported by a growing number of collectors with smaller purses. This, in turn, encouraged the growth of businesses that specialised in importing books from Europe, such as those of the Stevens, Sabin, and Denham families, as well as of specialist booksellers in America, including George D. Smith and Rosenbach.[17] In 1914 the London-based (Polish-Lithuanian-born) dealer Wilfrid Voynich followed in Alfred Quaritch's footsteps, bringing an exhibition of books to the United States, which he took to Washington, Baltimore, New York, Philadelphia, Minneapolis, Cleveland, and Chicago. In addition to courting individuals, Voynich exhibited his books at museums and galleries, selling illuminated manuscripts to The Art Institute of Chicago.[18] Business was good enough that Voynich opened an office in New York, making regular trips to

University, Plimpton MS 111; New York, Morgan Library, M.8, M.23, M.43, M.95, M.125, M.179, M.946; San Marino, Huntington Library, HM 1104.

[15] London, Bernard Quaritch Ltd., American Customers Book; C. Q. Wrentmore, 'Foreword', in *A Catalogue of Books and Manuscripts Issued to Commemorate the One Hundredth Anniversary of the Firm of Bernard Quaritch 1847–1947* (London: Bernard Quaritch, 1947), pp. xv–xvi.

[16] 'Donations Outstrip All Previous Years', *The Chicago Tribune*, 1 January 1901, p. 22.

[17] See D. C. Dickinson, *Dictionary of American Antiquarian Bookdealers* (Westport: Greenwood Press, 1998).

[18] 'Coming Exhibitions', *Bulletin of the Art Institute of Chicago*, 9(6) (October 1915), p. 78; 'The Voynich Collection', *Bulletin of the Art Institute of Chicago*, 9(7) (November 1915), p. 97; 'Illuminated Manuscripts', *Bulletin of the Art Institute of Chicago*, 10(2) (February 1916), p. 144.

Europe to obtain more stock.[19] Likewise, American collectors continued to seek
books in Europe, and London remained the centre of the increasingly international rare book trade.

Book auctions and sales of whole libraries (*en bloc*) were reported
in the press on both sides of the Atlantic, albeit often with different
emphasis. In 1902 the London *Times* lamented the sale of the library of
the Briton, Richard Bennett, to an anonymous American, while in
response *The New York Times* named the purchaser as Morgan, observing 'Mr. Morgan's library is rapidly becoming the most valuable
private book collection in the world'.[20] In 1911, the decision to auction
Hoe's library in New York irritated European dealers, who never-
theless crossed the Atlantic for the sales. Yet Hoe's executors were
justified as Smith, acting as Huntington's agent as well as buying for
his own stock, in competition with Morgan and others, paid large sums
for books, setting a new record of $50,000 for a Gutenberg Bible.[21]
According to one American newspaper, this prompted 'renewed lamen-
tations at London, Paris and Berlin over the unconscionable rapacity
of the American millionaires who are robbing Europe of its treasures
of art and antiquity and even its treasures of literature'.[22] In Europe,
such attitudes were underpinned by the idea that as none of the books
had been made in America, collectors there had less claim to them
than Europeans, whilst American authors celebrated their nation's
contemporary wealth and power.

The record price for the Gutenberg Bible was reported in the British
press, but London papers still managed to champion British dealers, for
example noting that 'Mr. Quaritch secured one exquisite Horae [Book of

[19] Papers from the New York office are preserved at the Grolier Club, New York;
see also J. W. Thompson, 'Wilfrid Michael Voynich', *Progress of Medieval
Studies in the United States and Canada* (1931), pp. 90–2.

[20] 'Pierpont Morgan and Caxton', *NYT*, 5 July 1902, p. 21.

[21] See D. C. Dickinson, 'Mr. Huntington and Mr. Smith', *The Book Collector*, 37(3)
(1988), p. 374.

[22] 'The Most Wonderful Bible in the World', *The Buffalo Sunday Morning News*,
14 May 1911, p. 19.

Hours] with microscopic illuminations for only $975'.[23] Moreover, London was not running short of books. The year 1911 also saw the start of the sale at Sotheby's in London of the library of Henry Huth and his son Alfred Henry, a process that took eight years, while sales of parts of the enormous library amassed by Sir Thomas Phillipps in the nineteenth century were held at Sotheby's throughout the period 1890–1929 and beyond.[24] In the twentieth century Quaritch's commission books included many pages of entries from American clients including Huntington and Folger for these sales. By 1914, Smith ventured onto the London market, sending triumphant reports of his large expenditure to the American press. After the auction of the Earl of Pembroke's library in 1914, at which Smith reportedly spent $100,000, *The New York Times* claimed that the '"Squeal of English" at Losing Treasures to Americans Amuses Him'.[25] Not content with creating a stir in London's auction rooms, Smith bought part of the library of the Dukes of Devonshire *en bloc* in 1914 and that of the Earls of Ellesmere in 1917.[26] Although there were some expressions of regret in the British press, these were tempered by the economic reality that the money was extremely welcome to the British sellers.

The close relationship between the British and American participants in the book trade, publicised in *The Book Lover* in 1889, found another expression in 1925, in a pair of articles that sought to nuance the standard narratives about the trade. The first, written by Henry Mencken and published in *The American Mercury* in January 1925, argued for greater empathy with the English, who were parting with their treasures.[27] He argued that books made in England should remain there, where they were more likely to receive study and where they would find buyers if Americans

---

[23] 'The Hoe Library Sale: Keen Competition', *The Times*, 3 May 1911, p. 5; for the Gutenberg Bible see *Westminster Gazette*, 1 May 1911, p. 4.

[24] See A. N. L. Munby, *The Dispersal of the Phillipps Library*, Phillipps Studies 5 (Cambridge: Cambridge University Press, 1960).

[25] 'Pembroke Books Fetch $194,680', *NYT*, 27 June 1914, p. 3.

[26] F. Herrmann, *Sotheby's: Portrait of an Auction House* (London: Chatto & Windus, 1980), pp. 125–6.

[27] H. L. Mencken and G. J. Nathan, 'Clinical Notes', *The American Mercury*, January 1925, p. 57.

did not inflate prices. Moreover, Mencken suggested that 'this inordinate hogging of books [. . .] must have, in the long run, an evil effect upon British-American relations'. In response, Clement King Shorter, writing in the British paper *The Sphere*, produced counterarguments. As a collector, who might want to sell, Shorter was pleased that Americans were raising the price for rare books. Moreover, he declared 'My own feeling with regard to book-collecting is that we are one people', suggesting that he saw books as potentially playing a role in international relations by reinforcing the cultural power of a shared heritage. Shorter also claimed that a 'great many of the books sold to America come back to England'.[28] This may have been optimistic, but it was echoed by Rosenbach, who in 1927 argued that the British could buy back their books from shops in Philadelphia, New Orleans, Minneapolis, and San Francisco, incidentally evoking a much wider geographical spread of the trade than had been described by either Alfred Quaritch's 1890 tour or Voynich's travels in 1914–1915.[29]

In contrast to the abundant supply of rare books at auction in Britain, fuelled in part by a series of Settled Land Acts in the 1880s that made it possible for individuals to apply to the Court of Chancery to sell items that formed part of an entailed estate, in the 1890s manuscripts and early printed books were less common in American sales.[30] Moreover, when such items did appear, typically in New York or Boston, the prices raised were low. In 1891, the sale of Ives' library raised $124,366.25, well short of the estimated $160,000 that Ives had spent on his books.[31] In particular, the Pembroke Hours, a fifteenth-century illuminated manuscript which sold for $5,900, had cost Ives $10,000.[32] The sale of Augustin Daly's library in 1900 was

---

[28] C. K. S[horter], 'A Literary Letter: The Solidarity of Book-Collecting', *The Sphere*, 10 January 1925, p. 38.

[29] Rosenbach, 'Why America Buys', p. 459.

[30] See P. Mandler, *The Fall and Rise of the Stately Home* (New Haven: Yale University Press, 1997), pp. 123–4; M. Purcell, *The Country House Library* (New Haven: Yale University Press, 2017), pp. 250–2.

[31] 'Some Costly Books', *The Buffalo Commercial*, 10 March 1891, p. 7.

[32] 'Costly Books at Auction', *The New York Sun*, 7 March 1891, p. 3. The manuscript is now Philadelphia Museum of Art, 1945–65–2.

hailed by the American press as proof that New York was now 'a better market than London', but failed to attract European buyers.[33] Strikingly, both Irwin and Lefferts chose to sell their collections *en bloc*, in 1900 and 1901 respectively, through the New York dealer George H. Richmond rather than risk auction sales.[34] The Hoe sales in 1911 and 1912 were significant in raising prices comparable with Europe, but supply in America continued to be much smaller than that available in Europe.

The growing trade in New York employed a glamour lacking from London's business-like auction rooms. John Carter described the extraordinary setting of American book auctions:

> American sales were held in a very different style from London's: usually in the evening, with a fashionable crowd at any important dispersal; comfortable chairs, and uniformed staff calling bids for the auctioneer; a spotlight on the lot selling, which is reverently displayed on a dais (no passing round the table); in short, an atmosphere eminently conducive to the painless extraction of that extra bid.[35]

In 1912, an American commentator incisively described the setting of a sale at the Anderson Auction Company as 'more like a theatre than a place of business, perhaps more like a church than a theatre'.[36] In contrast, photographs of Lord Amherst's sale at Sotheby's in London in 1908 showed dealers and collectors packed into a small room around the horseshoe-shaped table, many having to stand. The American settings for auctions contributed to the idea that the acquisition of rare books

---

[33] 'Daly Book Sale Results', *The New York Sun*, 22 April 1900, p. 17.

[34] 'Big Sale of Rare Books', *NYT*, 30 March 1900, p. 14; *A Check-List of the Library of Mr. Marshall C. Lefferts [. . .] Purchased and for Sale by George H. Richmond* (New York: no publisher, 1901).

[35] J. Carter, *Taste and Technique in Book-Collecting: A Study of Recent Developments in Great Britain and the United States* (Cambridge: Cambridge University Press, 1948), p. 131.

[36] G. Burgess, 'The Battle of the Books', *Collier's Magazine*, 10 February 1912, p. 17.

and art works was a social, aesthetic, and cultural activity as well as a financial one.

In the 1890s the trade worked on the basis that £1 was equivalent to $5. However, following Britain's departure from the gold standard in 1919 the exchange rate fell to below $4 to the pound, and although the pound recovered by the end of the decade, buying books in London became very good value for Americans immediately after the First World War.[37] In addition, books 'which shall have been printed and bound or manufactured more than twenty years at the date of importation', were exempt from American import tariffs.[38] The date of books was not always straightforward to determine as old books were often rebound. On Alfred Quaritch's second visit to America in 1891 his father wrote to confirm 'all the bindings are above 20 years old of the books & MSS. shipped to you'.[39] Similarly, the lists of books brought to New York by Voynich detail which are in old bindings, new bindings, and 'secondhand bindings which have been made within the last 20 years'.[40] This Element ends with the Wall Street Crash in 1929, which triggered a global economic depression, underlining how important the American economy had become.

Reflecting on the book trade in 1924, a writer for the British magazine *The Tatler* remarked: 'It would be interesting to know if there is any difference in the value of *objets d'art* in their original settings and when they are transplanted'.[41] A short study like this one cannot hope to discuss every rare book that crossed the Atlantic in this period or every person involved in the trade. Rather than attempting a comprehensive history, this

---

[37] See A. O'Neill, 'Prices and Exchange Rates', in G. Mandelbrote (ed.), *Out of Print & Into Profit: A History of the Rare and Secondhand Book Trade in Britain in the Twentieth Century* (London: British Library, 2006), pp. 333–5.

[38] J. M. Carson, *The Tariff Act of 1890, compared with the Tariff Act of 1883 and the Mills Bill* (Washington, DC: Government Printing Office, 1891), p. 42.

[39] Oxford, Bodleian Library, MS Eng. Lett. c. 435, f. 151.

[40] New York, Grolier Club, Wilfrid Voynich Papers, London House Invoices, 1921–23, list of Rare Books and Manuscripts to be sent on the SS. Baltic, 14 October 1922, dated 12 October 1922.

[41] 'The Letters of Evelyn', *The Tatler*, 16 April 1924, p. 93.

Element approaches the trade in rare books between Britain and the United States from three angles, to assess how the same events were used to construct different histories in the two nations, with the aim of providing a framework for future research. Section 1 examines American perspectives. The lack of surviving documentation for the motivations of collectors including Morgan, Huntington, and Walters has led to a reliance on published sources, most of which have presented collecting as a heroic activity demonstrating the financial, aesthetic, and social superiority of these men. In addition, dealers including Smith and Rosenbach used press coverage to advertise themselves, presenting a carefully managed view of the trade. Yet beyond the headlines dissenting voices, including Mencken's, can be found in the American press, and claims made in newspapers can sometimes be compared against letters and records of purchases, such as those kept by Morgan's librarian Belle da Costa Greene and her staff.[42] Section 2 explores the views of the trade found in British sources, arguing that despite some calls for restrictions on the transatlantic trade, the interests of British sellers continued to be prioritised. Again, unpublished sources shed light on the complexity of the trade and the competing economic and cultural arguments within it. Section 3 addresses the 'book-brokers' operating in both Britain and America who facilitated the trade in rare books, but who have often been overshadowed by collectors. It argues that dealers played a significant role in matching books with clients and making a case for the purchase of specific items, as well as fulfilling services including providing advice on books and estimates of prices, bidding for items at auction, arranging transportation of books and valuing items for probate. The combined activities of buyers, sellers, and dealers determined the fate of rare books and helped shape attitudes towards them as part of developing cultural histories. Investigating the trade from these three perspectives thus demonstrates the varied values that were projected onto books as they passed through different contexts.

---

[42] On Greene see: H. Ardizzone, *An Illuminated Life: Belle da Costa Greene's Journey for Prejudice to Privilege* (New York: W. W. Norton, 2007).

1 American Perspectives

In June 1911, the American magazine *Puck* published a cartoon entitled 'The Magnet' (Figure 1). At the upper right of the image, J. Pierpont Morgan holds a magnet in the form of a dollar sign, with which he attracts the world's treasures, including books, to New York. The modern sky-scrapers that flank Morgan contrast with the antiquities attracted by the magnet, suggesting that the young nation is now able to acquire the historic cultural objects of older countries. The power of the dollar is presented as inescapable force and the inclusion of the American flag in Morgan's hat suggests that his activities benefit not just himself and New York, but potentially the whole nation. Indeed, that Morgan's collecting was consid-ered worthy of a cartoon indicates that he was recognised as one of a group of collectors building unprecedented collections of art and books. The image was humorous, but not hostile.

Echoing the wealth of material displayed in the cartoon, in 1922 the dealer Abraham Rosenbach told *The Publishers' Weekly*: 'It is now dawning upon us that we have been living in the most wonderful period of opportunity that book collectors have ever had'.[43] Just two years later, Henry Mencken called for a re-examination of American book collecting, arguing that American collectors were having a corrosive influence on the wider book market, on Anglo-American relations and even on scholarship.[44] Mencken was a rare dissenting voice in press reports that celebrated the activities of American collectors and dealers, but his article provides insights into the complexity and potential impact of the trade in rare books between Britain and America, as well as the different perspectives of some of those within it.

1.1 Hands across the Sea

In 1925, under the heading 'Hands across the sea' Mencken set out what he saw as an interlinked set of problems with contemporary American activity in the English book market. Focusing on books that had been produced in

---

[43] F. M. Hopkin, 'The Golden Age of Book Collecting: An Interview with Dr. Rosenbach', *PW*, 28 October 1922, p. 1542.

[44] Mencken and Nathan, 'Clinical Notes', pp. 56–7.

Figure 1 U. J. Keppler, 'The Magnet', *Puck*, 21 June 1911

England, he explained that 'the books that the agents of American profiteers now gobble so copiously in London are not merely old books; they are, in many cases, national treasures of the English people. Some of them are quite unique; when the single known copy comes to American there is none left for England'.[45] He went on,

> Even when such books reach our public libraries they are not where they belong. They ought to be in the libraries of England. England produced them and England ought to have them. To set up any contrary doctrine is to argue that there is no such thing as a national treasure – that everything belongs, as of right, to whoever offers the most money for it.[46]

This view resonates with the cartoon of Morgan with his magnet, attracting the treasures of other nations with the powerful dollar. Instead, Mencken argued that Americans, rather than benefitting from London's post-war economy, should refrain from increasing prices by participating in the market, to allow the British to buy books. In this context Mencken saw the presence of an American at London auctions as 'a constant affront to English sensibilities. He visualizes the superior wealth of the Republic – the only country which made a profit out of the war'.[47] Mencken added, 'The English may be polite to him, but they detest and despise him in their hearts. He is, to them, simply a barbarian on a raid'.

For Mencken American economic dominance applied without restraint was particularly undesirable for the American collector who, 'as a rule, is extravagantly Anglomaniacal; he craves English good will'. He went on to argue that there were no 'logical reasons for bringing such treasures to America'. Explaining:

> America did not produce them, and Americans in general are not interested in them, save as things costing a lot of money. Moreover, there are very few scholars in this

[45] Ibid., 56. [46] Ibid., 57. [47] Ibid.

country capable of studying them to any profit; the over-
whelming majority of such students are Englishmen, and
live in England. Yet more, there is no sign, so far, that the
profiteers who buy them have any intention of putting them
at the disposal of such scholars as we have. Now and then,
true enough, a Morgan library is opened, or it is announced
that a Huntington library is to be opened at some vague time
in the future, but in the main the profiteers hoard their loot
very carefully, and so it has no public value whatever.

In Mencken's view,

The thing that makes news is not the fact that another
unique example of incunabula has come to America; the
news lies in the fact that a prodigious and unprecedented
price has been paid for it – that all possible English compe-
titors have been knocked out by an American who is willing
to pay twice what the book is worth for the childish satisfaction of grabbing it and hoarding it. The collections of such
men are not, properly speaking libraries; they are simply
safe deposit vaults full of sunbursts.

At the other end of the spectrum, there were American collectors who
felt strongly that there *were* logical reasons for bringing English book
treasures to America. When George Watson Cole described the
Huntington Library in 1923, he felt no need to justify the English holdings:
'the Huntington Library has not only acquired many of the rarest books in
the English language but copies in the finest possible condition, or those that
the most eminent English collectors have for many decades selected to grace
their shelves'.[48] In late-nineteenth and early-twentieth-century America,
some found security in a widespread ideological narrative of entitlement to
English objects of cultural and historic significance. Contemporary voices

[48] G. W. Cole, *The Henry E. Huntington Library and Art Gallery* (New York:
R. R. Bowker, 1923), p. 5.

frequently expressed a strong belief that American identity, nationalism, and even progress were rooted in an English past. Ralph Waldo Emerson voiced this sentiment in his popular *English Traits*, writing that 'England, an old and exhausted island, must one day be contented, like other parents, to be strong only in her children'.[49] Americans traveling to Britain in the nineteenth century often described the experience as a kind of homecoming, with American tourists flocking to various literary landmarks. Nathaniel Hawthorne wrote in *Our Old Home* that England felt so familiar to him that it may represent, 'the print of a recollection in some sort of ancestral mind'.[50] And Henry James declared himself 'most haunted with the London of Dickens, [. . .] as if it were still recoverable, still exhaling its queerness in patches perceptible to the appreciative'.[51]

James extended that sense of familiarity to feelings of proprietorship. Declaring London 'the capital of the human race', James suggested that Americans were in a unique position to fully appreciate England: 'it takes passionate pilgrims, vague aliens, and other disinterested persons to appreciate the "points" of this admirable country'.[52] Collectively, these voices reveal a strong emotional attachment to English heritage. Yet, significantly, that heritage could represent social exclusion as vigorously as inclusion. Mencken, for example, read some forms of Anglophilia as class signifiers in *The American Language*, writing that: lacking 'a native aristocracy of any settled position and authority, persons of social pretensions are thrown back upon English usage and opinion for guidance, and the vocabulary and pronunciation of the West End of London naturally flavor their speech'.[53] Perhaps unavoidably, as the twentieth century progressed, and America continued to strengthen economically, an increasingly pressing

[49] R. W. Emerson, *English Traits and Representative Men* (Boston: Phillips, Sampson, 1856), pp. 274–5.

[50] N. Hawthorne, *Our Old Home, and English Note-Books* (Boston: Houghton, Mifflin, 1902), p. 83.

[51] H. James, *English Hours* (Boston: Houghton, Mifflin, 1905), p. 35.

[52] Ibid., 13, 76.

[53] H. L. Mencken, *The American Language* (New York: Alfred A. Knopf, 1937), p. 265.

intellectual concern surfaced over whether America would ultimately represent an extension of the English national identity or a sharp departure. Stephen Spender reflected on the seriousness of this matter, writing that for some individuals it was a 'matter of life and death', even as there was considerable debate over which – the British past or the American future – represented death.[54] Spender summarised the debate, in a description that resonates with 'The Magnet' cartoon:

> For there was always at the back of all other American calculations the certainty that the American future would 'replace' the European past. This might mean that America would accumulate traditions of its own, or it might mean that it would transport European masterpieces [...] to America in such enormous quantities that it would be found to have annexed the European tradition, in stone and libraries and on canvas; or, again, it might mean that it would realize in unprecedented architectural forms and in technology the end-process of Progress swallowing up the tail of the tradition, replacing it with that many-storeyed dragon, New York.[55]

What Spender makes clear is the necessity of considering emotional and financial investments in English heritage through the lens of contemporary America. As T. J. Jackson Lears explains, 'so many collectors were forward-looking millionaires', whose tastes 'stemmed from emotional needs as well as intellectual fashion'.[56] Moreover, collecting 'the art of the past could buttress one's prestige in the present'.[57] In sum, the accumulation of English cultural treasures enabled the American collector to lay claim to

---

[54] S. Spender, *Love-Hate Relations: English and American Sensibilities* (London: Hamish Hamilton, 1974), p. xi.

[55] Ibid., 4.

[56] T. J. Jackson Lears, *No Place of Grace: Antimodernism and the Transformation of American Culture, 1880–1920* (New York: Pantheon Books, 1981), pp. 187–8.

[57] Ibid., 187.

a specific historical narrative, to anticipate the direction of American cultural developments, and to establish their own social credentials. This was never more evident than in the activities of leading American book clubs.

Throughout this period, the Grolier Club was 'the leading force in bibliographical work and publication in America'.[58] In 1902 the Club published *One Hundred Books Famous in English Literature*, overseen by George Edward Woodberry, which quickly became an influential shopping list for collectors. Even in 1931 one commentator noted that dealers often referred to *One Hundred Books* as the 'list made a deep impression upon collectors both in America and in England'.[59] Woodberry's enthusiasm for English literature is as remarkable as it is revealing. Woodberry insisted that books were the physical embodiments of national thinking, that: 'The eye rests on these hundred titles of books famous in English literature [. . .] and sees in miniature the intellectual conformation of a nation'.[60] Arguing for the universality of English literary texts, Woodberry wrote that national books 'must be English books, not in tongue only, but body and soul'.[61] He claimed Shakespeare as 'the greatest of our writers' and the English Bible as 'the greatest of our books', stating that 'if no more were to be written on the page of English, yet what is written there, contained and handed down in famous books [. . .] will constitute a moral dominion'.[62] Woodberry's confidence in the appeal of English books on historical, cultural, and intellectual grounds was such that he neglected to provide sufficient bibliographical justifications for acquiring these specific volumes, and a second catalogue had to be published the following year.[63] Nonetheless, Woodberry's landmark

---

[58] W. A. Jackson, 'America', in *The Bibliographical Society, 1892–1942: Studies in Retrospect* (London: Bibliographical Society, 1949), p. 186.

[59] B. W. Currie, *Fishers of Books* (Boston: Little, Brown, 1931), p. 108.

[60] *One Hundred Books Famous in English Literature* (New York: Grolier Club, 1902), p. xiii.

[61] Ibid., xiv. [62] Ibid., xlv, lii.

[63] *Bibliographical Notes on One Hundred Books Famous in English Literature* (New York: Grolier Club, 1903), p. viii.

list became 'the simplest plan – and the costliest – that might be followed by the very busy business man collector'.[64] Moreover, his 'Introduction' offered generations of collectors a convenient 'summing up of both literary values and permanent worth from a bibliomaniac's peculiar viewpoint'.[65] Those American businessmen with outwardly the very simplest plans – to quickly acquire the finest books possible at any cost – became a particular focus of interest for an American public increasingly fascinated by expensive art collections and for those engaged with questions of heritage and national identity.

1.2 The Dizzy Heights of Dollardom

Between 1890 and 1929 the number of both rare English books and other books and manuscripts purchased by Americans only increased, reaching what a British commentator described as the 'dizzy heights of dollardom'.[66] By the late 1920s, Rosenbach estimated that fifty per cent of the purchases made by British dealers made their way eventually into American collections.[67] English books were important enough that American collectors sought them out even when it was challenging and risky to do so. In the Grolier Club's 1893 *Catalogue of Original and Early Editions of English Writers*, the 'Preface' begins:

> It is an undoubted fact that the increasing study of English literature has [. . .] developed new interest in the original editions of those authors whose writings form the foundation of that literature. This is true not only of England but also of America, where the eagerness of buyers for this class of books bears witness to the truth of the statement [. . .] American collectors of old English literature are not very numerous, though their number is constantly increasing, but

---

[64] Currie, *Fishers*, p. 108. [65] Ibid.

[66] 'Collecting Modern Books: Prices, Pleasures and Pitfalls in the First-Edition Hobby', *The Graphic*, 22 August 1931, p. 272.

[67] A. S. W. Rosenbach, *Books and Bidders: The Adventures of a Bibliophile* (London: George Allen & Unwin, 1927), p. 257.

it seems just to add that for enthusiasm and devotion they
are not excelled by any class of collectors in the land.[68]

For these American collectors enthusiasm was an absolute require-
ment, as they faced disadvantages: being far from the London market and
'suffering further in not having at command for comparison and study the
vast treasures contained in the British Museum and other English public
libraries'.[69] As a consequence of having limited access to the London book
market, Americans had been 'easily disappointed by the catalogues of
some English booksellers and auctioneers whose tendency to over-
describe and quietly omit all mention of imperfections has been unfortunately but too common'.[70] A few years earlier Bernard Quaritch had
addressed the problem of inaccurate catalogue entries and its impact on
American collectors. His 1886 *Catalogue of Manuscripts* opened with
a remarkable statement:

> It is claimed for this catalogue that the descriptions are as
> faithful and as nearly correct as a tolerable experience of
> MSS., combined with a sincere desire to be exact, could
> make them. At the very least, that reckless blundering is
> avoided which is only too common in contemporary cata-
> logues, and which is nearly as pernicious as a wilful inten-
> tion to deceive. Instances of this practice are numerous, and
> must cause bitter regret amongst distant purchasers, espe-
> cially at auctions, who have charged irresponsible and inex-
> perienced agents with their commissions.[71]

Quaritch then described three examples of buyers being seriously misled by
English catalogues. The first was a manuscript which 'brought such a high
price in consequence of a note in a catalogue which stated that it had been

---

[68] *Catalogue of Original and Early Editions of Some of the Poetical and Prose Works of
English Writers* (New York: Grolier Club, 1893), p. vii.

[69] Ibid., vii–viii.   [70] Ibid., viii.

[71] *Catalogue of Manuscripts: Illuminated and Remarkable Examples, from the Ninth to
the Sixteenth Century*, no. 369 (London: Bernard Quaritch, 1886), p. 237.

the property of St. Louis in A.D. 1248'. The second was advertised as a 'Livre d'Heures which had belonged to Mary Queen of Scots, and had been used by her on the scaffold'. And the final manuscript was described in a catalogue as the prayer book of Margaret of Anjou. Unfortunately, none of this turned out to be true. The first manuscript was of a later date, the second manuscript was in reality a 'Flemish book of little value', and the ownership of the final manuscript was 'a gratuitous mis-statement, based upon the circumstance that some person had fancied a resemblance between one of the miniatures representing the Virgin and an old picture of that Queen'.[72] All three manuscripts currently reside in American libraries, and at various points were owned by members of the Grolier Club.[73] It was not without reason that Rosenbach described the collecting of manuscripts as 'the branch of the collector's game that is most difficult'.[74]

Yet despite being geographically remote from the London trade, and the complications that involved, American buying only increased over time in both volume and expenditure. Reflecting on book buying from the vantage point of the 1920s, Rosenbach pointed out that: 'According to some of the English newspapers that bewail the loss to England of her greatest monuments of the past, it is a new thing, this interest in things English on part of the American public. On the contrary, it has been going on, increasing in volume, it is true, from about the year 1840'.[75] In 1902 *The New York Times* published an article declaring that 'our bibliographical invasion of England has not ceased'.[76] By 1914, a *New York Times* headline triumphantly read: 'England's Rarest Books Being Bought by Americans', announcing that,

---

[72] Ibid.

[73] The manuscripts are now: Harvard, Houghton Library, MS Richardson 1; San Marino, Huntington Library, HM 1200; New York, Morgan Library, M.1000.

[74] A. S. W. Rosenbach, *Henry C. Folger as a Collector* (New Haven: privately printed, 1931), p. 27.

[75] Rosenbach, *Books and Bidders*, p. 243; S. Gwara, 'Peddling Wonderment, Selling Privilege: Launching the Market for Medieval Books in Antebellum New York', *Perspectives médiévales*, 41 (2020).

[76] 'England's Shakespearean Losses', *NYT*, 16 August 1902, p. 13.

'Some of Most Valuable Treasures of Famed Huth Collection of Scarce Books Are Latest Booty Wrested from England by American Buyers'.[77]

Press reports were very precise about prices paid (or supposedly paid) for items. Within the coverage of the Hoe sale were lists of prices paid for books and their purchasers. Entries from 2 May 1911 read: 'Illuminated "Horae" of the fifteenth century, probably executed in the North of France, $2,300 (Smith.)' and 'Illuminated "Horae" of the fifteenth century, a brilliant manuscript, apparently painted by a Flemish artist under French influence. $3,000 (Maggs.)'.[78] Offering no further physical description of these manuscripts, of their provenance, or explaining their high value to any satisfactory degree, readers were left understanding only their monetary worth and the name of the individual able to afford them, or of their agent. Interested readers could compare the reports with the more detailed sale catalogues, but the profusion of newspaper articles throughout the early twentieth century containing information of this nature – light in bibliographical and historical detail – suggests that readers were receiving the information that most interested them. Headlines about major sales frequently included price figures, for example '$6,300 for Manuscript Bible' or '$322,500 Paid to Save Rare Books to Britain'.[79] Yet Rosenbach claimed that for the most devoted collectors, monetary value was, 'the last as well as the least important place in his passion for collecting'.[80]

1.3 The Prince of Book Collectors

The New York Times' article about American success at the Huth sale of 1914 provided a list of leading American collectors of recent years including: William Van Antwerp, Harry Elkins Widener, Huntington, Morgan, E. Dwight Church, John Gribbel, Beverly Chew, Grenville Kane, Ward

---

[77] 'England's Rarest Books Being Bought by Americans', *NYT*, 12 July 1914, p. 7.

[78] 'Morgan Pays $42,800 for Book at Hoe Sale', *NYT*, 2 May 1911, p. 2; the manuscript bought by Smith is now San Marino, Huntington Library, HM 1099.

[79] '$6,300 for Manuscript Bible', *NYT*, 17 May 1901, p. 5; '$322,500 Paid to Save Rare Books to Britain', *NYT*, 30 July 1929, p. 14.

[80] Rosenbach, *Books and Bidders*, p. 44.

Hill Lamon, Robert Hoe, William A. White, Marsden Perry, Henry Folger Jr, Harry Smith, George Plimpton, Francis Wilson, and W. Loring Andrews.[81] These were just the more prominent names in American collecting. A 1913 article claimed that American 'Book-collectors are said to abound; their number mounts into the hundreds'.[82] Some of these collectors appear to have been spending heavily: in 1907 *The New York Times* reported that there were at least six private libraries in New York worth between one and two million dollars.[83] No American collector, however, captured widespread media interest as Morgan, Folger, and Huntington did. When the first authorised description of Morgan's library appeared in 1908, following the completion of the new building in 1906, *The New York Times'* headline read 'Morgan called a genius' and the article declared that: 'Morgan is probably the greatest collector of things splendid and beautiful and rare who has ever lived'.[84] In 1917, four years after Morgan's death, the paper announced: 'Huntington Now the Premier Book Collector', granting him the title 'Prince of Book Collectors'.[85] And by 1919, the paper observed that Folger, 'owns what is regarded as the finest library of Shakespeareana in America'.[86] John Carter would later note that 'All three men became magnets for the attraction of likely books from dealers and private owners throughout the world'.[87]

It was no accident that Morgan and Huntington were the only named individuals in Mencken's attack on American collectors. By 1908, an anonymous English author of a *New York Times* article opined of Morgan's recently completed library:

---

[81] 'England's Rarest Books', p. M7.

[82] F. A. King, 'The Complete Collector', *The Bookman*, 36(5) (January 1913), p. 510.

[83] 'Private Libraries in New York That Have Cost Large Fortunes', *NYT*, 7 April 1907, p. 5.

[84] 'Mr. Morgan's Great Library', *NYT*, 4 December 1908, p. 1.

[85] 'Huntington Now the Premier Book Collector', *NYT*, 27 May 1917, p. 63.

[86] 'Folger Paid Record Price', *NYT*, 28 October 1919, p. 8.

[87] Carter, *Taste*, p. 35.

> I do not believe that any one in England knows how many
> things that ought never to have left the country are con-
> tained in these few cubic yards of space in New York. [. . .]
> I think that these heirlooms of England will never go back,
> and, I repeat, they should never have come here.[88]

In the years that followed, Huntington made headlines through his tenacious pursuit of English libraries and rare books, forming a reputation as 'the most formidable rival to collectors of English literature' by dominating 'as perhaps no other single collector has done before or since, a whole series of sales of outstanding importance'.[89] One of his most prominent purchases was that of the Bridgewater Library in 1917. Famous as one of the oldest and most significant private libraries in England, the Bridgewater collection was regarded as 'the most extensive collection of English literature in the world'.[90] It was widely reported in the press that Huntington had spent $1,000,000 on the library, with George D. Smith acting as his agent. For this remarkable price, Huntington acquired a collection of more than 20,000 items, including 8,000 books, 200 manuscripts, and more than 10,000 histor-ical documents.[91] Leaving England inside 101 crates, American readers – who would have been aware of the threat posed to ships by German submarines – were told that the library was the largest single shipment of books ever to cross the Atlantic.[92] Within one of these crates, the fifteenth-century Ellesmere Chaucer made its way to California.[93] The book was described by *The New York Times* as, 'unquestionably the greatest monument of English literature in the world'.[94] It was valued at $50,000 – a remarkable figure,

---

[88] 'Mr. Morgan's Great Library', p. 2. [89] Carter, *Taste*, p. 35.

[90] 'H. E. Huntington Pays $1,000,000 for Bridgewater Library', *PW*, 26 May 1917, p. 1736.

[91] 'Famous Library Sold: Unknown Purchaser of the Bridgwater Collection', *The Times*, 17 May 1917, p. 7; Dickinson, 'Mr. Huntington and Mr. Smith', pp. 387–8.

[92] 'H. E. Huntington Pays $1,000,000', p. 1736. See also, 'George Smith Buys Bridgewater MSS', *NYT*, 18 May 1917, p. 5.

[93] Now San Marino, Huntington Library, MS EL 26 C 9.

[94] 'Rare Literary Gems for H. E. Huntington', *NYT*, 21 May 1917, p. 9.

matching the record price paid for the Gutenberg Bible at the Hoe sale.[95] *The New York Times* triumphantly reported that with the purchase of the Bridgewater library, Huntington's collection had likely become 'the finest in the world' and that 'nothing on so magnificent a scale has been known before in the world's history of book collecting'.[96] If there were American anxieties about the removal of a library of such national significance from England, it is not evident in the contemporary press. Nor were concerns publicly expressed when Huntington purchased the Kemble-Devonshire plays and Devonshire Caxtons in 1914. In fact, *The New York Times* responded directly to British complaints about the sale:

> *The London Times* finds consolation in the sudden discovery that these books have no 'spiritual' value, are not works of art, and should be classed as mere curios. [. . .] had these rare specimens of early typography found a resting place in the British Museum *The Times* would have taken a different view of their acquisition.[97]

This is not to suggest that Huntington never received criticism from the American press. In fact, Huntington launched his public collecting career with purchases that attracted negative attention. Huntington's name became widely associated with book-buying following the well-publicised 1911 Hoe sale – an event that would seem to represent so much of what Mencken found repugnant about the American book trade. The Hoe sale was a pivotal event for American buyers and dealers and was the first major American book sale to draw important European buyers, reportedly achieving sales figures, 'more than four times the largest amount ever received for a library in all the history of book sales by auction'.[98] Even as late as 1900 one writer had declared that 'those who know anything at all about these

---

[95] 'H. E. Huntington Pays $1,000,000', p. 1736.

[96] 'Rare Literary Gems', p. 9; 'Huntington Now the Premier Book Collector', p. 63.

[97] 'Decrying a Lost Bargain', *NYT*, 21 March 1914, p. 12.

[98] W. Towner, *The Elegant Auctioneers* (London: Victor Gollancz, 1971), p. 268; Burgess, 'Battle', p. 17.

matters do not need to be told that London is an infinitely better market [. . .] than New York'.[99] Describing the sale of the Augustin Daly library in New York, he claimed that the catalogue 'would be a credit to a third-rate provincial auctioneer', adding confidently that 'we believe that not a single English bookseller is attending the sale, but doubtless many of the lots will in due course find their way back to England'.[100] The Hoe sale – its polished catalogue overseen by Englishman Arthur Swann (but labelled 'primitive' by the British *Morning Post*) – would challenge such beliefs.[101] Initially, it was not certain that the sale would even take place in America: Hoe's will simply stipulated that the collection be sold in either London, Paris, or New York. London was the obvious choice, but the executors (one of whom happened to be the brother of influential collector, Beverly Chew) ultimately selected New York.[102] The executors must have had enough confidence in the American book market to risk what could have been a costly mistake. *Publishers' Weekly* quickly predicted that the sale, 'will bring the highest aggregate totals of any collection ever sold at auction, not only in America, but in the world, and that at least one of its literary treasures will bring a higher price than has ever before been realized for a single work in the public market', anticipating that at least ten manuscripts would sell for $10,000 each.[103] With Smith as his agent, Huntington did not disappoint expectations of record-breaking spending. When he purchased the Gutenberg Bible for $50,000 it was reported a few days later that, 'Mr. Huntington by this purchase succeeds J. Pierpont Morgan as the owner of the costliest book of the world'.[104] By the close of the final Hoe sale in November 1912, Huntington had purchased around $560,000 worth of books.[105] While others spent large sums at the Hoe sale, it was Huntington who, as a man willing to pay $50,000 for one book, received the most publicity for his spending – and the most criticism.

[99] 'The Augustin Daly Library', *The Athenæum*, no. 3778, 24 March 1900, p. 371.

[100] Ibid. [101] 'Our Critics Oversea' [*sic*], *NYT*, 12 November 1911, p. 30.

[102] Towner, *Elegant Auctioneers*, p. 262.

[103] 'Hoe Library Sale May Break Records', *PW*, 8 April 1911, p. 1500.

[104] 'The Hoe Sale', *PW*, 29 April 1911, p. 1794.

[105] D. C. Dickinson, *Henry E. Huntington's Library of Libraries* (San Marino: Huntington Library, 1995), p. 47.

In the immediate aftermath of the first Hoe sales, several important figures in the book world expressed concerns over the impact of such high prices on the market. Morgan's librarian, Belle Greene called the high prices at the Hoe sale 'perfectly ridiculous', adding 'they are most harmful and establish a dangerous precedent. [. . .] Things have been raised to a fictitious value'.[106] *The New York Times* indicated that the European dealers agreed, having stopped bidding, 'when prices begin to soar. They know a book's value and they are not going to pay more'.[107] Chicago dealer Walter Hill told the paper that the high prices paid are, 'in large measure due to Mr. Huntington and to ignorance of their real market value'.[108] The article with Hill's comments appeared next to one describing a man arrested for grand larceny after artificially inflating the prices of books and selling them to a trusting collector in Philadelphia.[109] A joke even circulated in the press that when a wife was asked whether her husband's purchase of a single book for $50,000 showed, 'how much you care for literature', she replied that it actually demonstrated 'how little we care for $50,000'.[110] In the period following the Hoe sale, American readers were given the impression that Huntington had done something shocking in spending so heavily, something that risked damaging public institutions, and something possibly foolish. The British *Morning Telegraph's* response to the sales – re-published in *The New York Times* – even appears to single out Huntington for comment (Huntington having made the bulk of his fortune in railroads): 'Soon the world of book collectors will have an opportunity of understanding the newer form of excitement [. . .] when old books were treated as if they were steel and rail shares'.[111] None of this press coverage, however, prevented Huntington from quickly establishing a secure place within the world of rare books, becoming remade as the 'Prince of Book Collectors'.

---

[106] 'J. P. Morgan's Librarian Says High Book Prices are Harmful', *NYT*, 30 April 1911, p. 13.

[107] Ibid.   [108] 'Prices at Hoe Sale Warmly Criticised', *NYT*, 28 April 1911, p. 24.

[109] 'Disappointed in Books', *NYT*, 28 April 1911, p. 24.

[110] 'Apropos of the Hoe Sale', *PW*, 17 June 1911, p. 2368.

[111] 'Our Critics Oversea' [*sic*], p. 30.

1.4 Books and Libraries

In June 1911, Huntington was invited to join the Grolier Club and shortly after that, he became one of the first members of the Hobby Club. Just as Huntington's stature grew within the community of book collectors, the American press moved quickly past the controversies of the Hoe sale. Whether Huntington's buying tactics at the Hoe sale had effectively damaged the rare book trade, the press offered no immediate answers. In addition to the high prices, Greene's observations on the sale had included that it 'is being sold practically en bloc' – a comment clearly meant to be critical of this method of large-scale, seemingly indiscriminate buying, and one clearly aimed at Huntington, who provided new competition for the Morgan collection. Shortly afterwards, Hoe's librarian, Carolyn Whipple, made a point of praising Hoe for his almost complete avoidance of *en bloc* buying.[112] *En bloc* buying was not unique to Huntington. Between 1899 and 1902, Morgan emerged as the pre-eminent American collector of books after purchasing three large libraries: that of the English bookseller James Toovey, the manuscripts from Theodore Irwin's library, and Richard Bennett's collection of rare books and manuscripts. The Bennett collection represented the largest purchase Morgan made for his library, and it is estimated to have cost Morgan at least $600,000 in 1902.[113] Similarly, Hoe purchased nearly all the library of Abbie Pope for an estimated $200,000–250,000 in 1895.[114]

In the cases of Morgan and Huntington, some of their most celebrated manuscripts – items the American press would turn to as demonstrative of their discerning taste – came to them through *en bloc* purchasing. Huntington acquired the Ellesmere Chaucer with the Bridgewater Library. And descriptions of Morgan's library during his lifetime frequently made reference to the thirteenth-century Huntingfield Psalter and the Golden Gospels of Henry VIII, both of which had been among the books

---

[112] '"Absurd" Prices at the Hoe Sale', *NYT*, 2 May 1911, p. 10.

[113] See F. H. Taylor, *Pierpont Morgan: As Collector and Patron* (New York: Pierpont Morgan Library, 1970), p. 20; Herrmann, *Sotheby's*, p. 120.

[114] 'News for Bibliophiles', *The Nation*, 30 March 1911, p. 315; Dickinson, *Dictionary of American Book Collectors*, p. 263.

exhibited by Quaritch in New York in 1890, coming to Morgan via the Bennett collection and the Irwin library respectively.[115] In 1902 *The New York Times* called the Huntingfield Psalter, 'a magnificent volume, containing a treasury of early English art such as can no longer be found (with this single exception) outside of the great public libraries'.[116] In 1908 the paper offered a slightly fuller account of the Golden Gospels: 'produced by an Anglo-Saxon scribe for Archbishop Wilfrid of York around 670, the manuscript (which features unusual purple vellum leaves) was presented to Henry VIII by the Pope around the time he received the title "Defender of the Faith"'.[117] Undoubtedly these were important and remarkable manuscripts, but for the general reader – fully aware the Morgan possessed a library full of rare treasures – it was never especially clear why these manuscripts merited attention above others. These were neither the oldest nor the most expensive manuscripts in Morgan's library.

Perhaps most revealingly, what the Ellesmere Chaucer, the Huntingfield Psalter, and the Golden Gospels share is the designation of being English cultural treasures. However, with the press magnifying the role of wealthy collectors above all other considerations, the acquisition of manuscripts became a narrative that could elicit feelings of national pride while avoiding thornier questions of entitlement. What emerged overall was a dual narrative regarding the acquisition of medieval manuscripts in early twentieth-century America: one circulating amongst members of the book world and a second, more laudatory, narrative filtered through the contemporary press. This second narrative not only made the public more aware of American collecting, but it blurred any distinction between rights to ownership and an ability to buy, contributing in part to the transformation of major private libraries into emergent centres of cultural authority. Morgan and Huntington were merely accumulating the material sources of American literary and historical thinking, and their cheque books entitled them to do so.

---

[115] Now New York, Morgan Library, M.43, M.23.

[116] 'Mr. Morgan's Books', *NYT*, 26 July 1902, p. 3.

[117] 'Mr. Morgan's Great Library', p. 2.

There are several explanations for how this public, more nationalistic narrative developed. Firstly, while there is plenty of evidence that American readers were interested in American collectors, there is less evidence that they were interested in the nuances of rare book collecting. Shortly after the Hoe sale, even *The New York Times* admitted that, 'The interest it excites among people who do not collect rare books is very mild, and extends not much further than the expression of astonishment over the payment of $50,000 for a Bible when a well-printed Bible may be bought for 50 cents'.[118] The 1913 version of *Books and Bookmen* included Andrew Lang's posthumous observation that, 'The world may not care very much about any man's mere books, but it is ready enough to hear about himself, whoever he is, if his name be well known'.[119] In 1908 *The Nation* declared that 'the publication in the London *Times* and *The New York Times* of an account of the library of J. Pierpont Morgan has naturally excited wide interest', but also noted that 'the catalogues of portions of his great library which have been printed by J. Pierpont Morgan, have scarcely been noticed by the public press'.[120] The article insisted that while the library itself drew some interest, most public attention stemmed from the fact that a celebrity financier was involved in the collecting. Even Rosenbach confessed in 1927 that, in spite of Huntington being, 'the greatest collector of books the world has ever known', with 'impeccable' taste in books, that 'America does not appreciate [the Huntington Library] to-day'.[121]

The New York Times suggested that, even for the collectors themselves, the context of collecting could matter more than the collected items:

> Some of the owners of these fine libraries have a genuine love of books. That is, however, only one of the motives that lead them to gather hundreds of manuscripts [. . .] The pleasure of possession counts for much. There is an element of profit in it, for a collector, if he knows how, can make his library as good

---

[118] 'The Hoe Sale', *NYT*, 26 April 1911, p. 12.

[119] A. Lang, *Books and Bookmen* (London: Longmans, Green, 1913), p. xi.

[120] 'Bibliophiles and Bibliophiles', *The Nation*, 87(2268), 3 December 1908, p. 596; 'News for Bibliophiles', *The Nation*, 87(2266), 3 December 1908, p. 545.

[121] Rosenbach, *Books and Bidders*, p. 253.

an investment as money spent on diamonds, railroad bonds, or Turkish rugs. Most of the collectors, however, enjoy the pleasures of acquisition for its adventures.[122]

It also helped that the context of collecting was widely accessible and generally entertaining, while bibliophilia could be difficult to identify with and the realities of the book trade complex, sometimes messy, even worse dull. Books did not always move in a neat line from England to America: sometimes items travelled back and forth before a buyer was found, repeatedly offered for sale. While the general American reader may have felt a sense of patriotic pride that Morgan was able to acquire the Huntingfield Psalter, those familiar with rare books were aware that for years the manuscript had failed to sell to anyone.

In June 1889 Bernard Quaritch put on a display of manuscripts at his shop in Piccadilly. Two of the manuscripts on display – the Huntingfield Psalter and the Towneley Mysteries – would go on to become important items in the collections of Morgan and Huntington respectively.[123] Both were offered for similar prices, the Huntingfield Psalter was advertised at £800 and the Towneley Mysteries, a rare example of English religious cycle drama, at £820. Neither manuscript sold and when Alfred Quaritch brought the Psalter to America the following year, he returned to London with the manuscript still unsold. The Psalter was bought by the British designer and socialist William Morris in 1895, whose collection was acquired by Bennett *en bloc* in 1897.[124] The Towneley Mysteries remained in Quaritch's stock for the rest of the nineteenth century and was eventually sold to the British stockbroker Sir Edward Coates. At the sale of his library in London in 1922 the manuscript was bought by Rosenbach, who sold it to Huntingdon.

If, as Mencken argued, American collectors were raiding barbarians, they appear to have been cautious raiders in 1890. Alfred Quaritch

---

[122] 'Private Libraries in New York', p. 5.

[123] The Towneley Mysteries is now San Marino, Huntington Library, HM 1.

[124] See Section 2.1.

described American collectors as excessively interested in bibliographical detail, price inflation, and their overall investment – hardly the image of voracious buyers interested only in books as expensive cultural trophies. Alfred's letters reveal that he made several direct attempts to persuade some of the leading American collectors to purchase the Huntingfield Psalter, without success. Perhaps this had something to do with the manuscript's condition. In one letter Alfred protested: 'People are devilish particular about condition of Books'.[125] Later, in 1910, *The New York Times* praised Hoe's manuscripts specifically for being 'as fresh and clean to-day as when they left their makers hands', stating that, 'the perfect preservation of those [manuscripts] in this collection seems little short of wonderful'.[126] However, when the Huntingfield Psalter appeared in Morgan's 1906 catalogue, it was described as having 'suffered severely from damp, which has caused the gold grounds of many of the pictures to flake off'.[127] Interestingly, this detail was absent from contemporary press publications.

Within the press coverage, Morgan was defined almost as much by what he rejected as what he acquired – and he was known for possessing the very finest art objects. Contemporary publications suggest there was limited public appetite for either bibliographical details or the contents of major rare book collections. The argument that the contents of Morgan's library were simply too extensive to describe repeatedly appeared in newspaper articles, biographical sketches, and even obituaries. *The New York Times* declared in 1913: 'to give even a list of the best of Mr. Morgan's treasures would take all of an issue'.[128] Carl Hovey's 1911 *The Life Story of J. Pierpont Morgan* claimed it would take 'a volume to enumerate and several volumes adequately to describe' Morgan's library. Using language that echoed a 1902

---

[125] London, Bernard Quaritch Ltd., letter from B. A. Quaritch to B. Quaritch, 10 March 1890.

[126] 'World's Finest Library Doomed to Destruction', *NYT*, 10 April 1910, p. 81.

[127] M. R. James, *Catalogue of Manuscripts and Early Printed Books from the Libraries of William Morris, Richard Bennett, Bertram Fourth Earl of Ashburnham, and Other Sources Now Forming Portion of the Library of J. Pierpont Morgan* (London: Chiswick Press, 1906), p. 33.

[128] 'Leading Collector of the Art World', *NYT*, 1 April 1913, p. 5.

New York Times article on the Bennett purchase, Hovey specifically mentioned only four medieval manuscripts: the Huntingfield Psalter, a 1380 Roman de la Rose, a 1485 Bourbon Book of Hours, and a Flemish Book of Hours bound for Mary Stuart.[129] With the notable exception of the Golden Gospels, the manuscripts acquired from Irwin rarely featured in discussions of the collection. Hovey was equally vague about Morgan's printed books, mentioning a Gutenberg Bible, a Mainz Psalter, and 'examples of the earliest press work'.[130] A similar insouciance appears in the work of Morgan's son-in-law, Herbert L. Satterlee, who devoted little attention to the contents of Morgan's library in his biographical writings.[131] Throughout the final years of his life, Morgan had attained sufficient celebrity for his movements and activities to be carefully monitored by the press. In 1906, tellingly, a *New York Times* article surfaced about his luggage being taken off an ocean liner ahead of other passengers. The missing commentary on Morgan's famous library is a notable absence in an otherwise well-documented life.

The nationalistic rhetoric of the press often filled a void left by the collectors themselves, who, even as their collections became increasingly well-known, could remain quite reticent about personal motivations. Shortly before his death, Morgan burned thirty years' worth of correspondences that would have shed incalculable light on his collecting.[132] Equally, there are few records of Huntington's personal views, and the evidence for Walters' manuscript acquisitions, let alone his motivations, is usually thin.[133] Huntington did grant an interview to John Daggett of the *Los Angeles Times* in January 1922, offering a rare insight into his collecting rationale:

---

[129] See 'Mr. Morgan's Books', p. 3; C. Hovey, *The Life Story of J. Pierpont Morgan* (New York: Sturgis & Walton, 1911), pp. 329–30; the manuscripts are probably now: New York, Morgan Library, M.43, M.132, M.179, M.231.

[130] Hovey, *Life Story*, p. 330.

[131] H. L. Satterlee, *J. Pierpont Morgan: An Intimate Portrait* (New York: Macmillan, 1930).

[132] L. H. Roth, 'J. Pierpont Morgan, Collector', in L. H. Roth (ed.), *J. Pierpont Morgan, Collector* (Wisbech: Balding and Mansell, 1987), p. 27.

[133] Dickinson, *Library of Libraries*, p. 262.

consolidate those private libraries which represent the life
efforts of notable connoisseurs [. . .]. Please do not mention
any monetary figure in connection with any books [. . .]
I say money has nothing to do with it. True value can
only be experienced in eons of time, by the march of
centuries to come and by the uplift of humanity.[134]

Nonetheless, stories about American titans of industry collecting spectacular European books for extravagant prices made good newspaper copy.
America was economically ascendent, leaving wealthy collectors well-
positioned to acquire what *they* perceived the nation to lack culturally,
historically, and artistically, or simply what appealed to them (or, in the case
of Morgan, to their trusted agents). Henry James best captured the prevail-
ing tone when, while visiting the Metropolitan Museum, he observed:
'There was money in the air, ever so much money [. . .] And the money
was to be all for the most exquisite things'.[135]

1.5 Motivations for Collecting

With American personal fortunes growing, and the possession of objects of
high culture becoming increasingly public and desirable, rapid institutional
development followed. In 1908, Walters was lauded for developing an art
gallery in Baltimore, and one commentator saw such activity as echoing an
idealised English custom in which 'the sons of the nobility largely deny
themselves the indulgence of leisure and of idle sport in order to devote
their lives to great questions of State policy or to other fields in which the
nation can be honorably served'.[136] America had no aristocracy, but as
Rosenbach observed in 1927, 'rare books and the precious things of the
collector follow the flow of gold'.[137] However, in terms of collectors'

---

[134] J. Daggett, 'Brings..His..Books..Here..By..Carloads..', *Los Angeles Times*,
9 January 1922, Part II, p. 1; Dickinson, *Library of Libraries*, p. 158.
[135] H. James, *The American Scene* (New York: Harper & Brothers, 1907), p. 186.
[136] 'Young Men and Art', *The Baltimore Sun*, 25 April 1908, p. 5.
[137] Rosenbach, *Books and Bidders*, p. 246.

motivations Rosenbach claimed that 'forming great libraries and art galleries solely for patriotic reasons [...] is perhaps after all a secondary consideration with them. Certainly it is not first'.[138] The British *Burlington Magazine* said as much about Morgan in 1913: 'Conquest was his joy; who can tell how much the desire for conquest was inspired in him by an instinctive feeling for the aesthetic needs of his country, and how much by the sheer delight in acquisition?'.[139] Yet even if collectors' motivations were not solely patriotic, Rosenbach labelled their activities 'magnificent' adding that the 'gathering of books in this country is in the hands of leaders of her industries' rather than scholars who 'make a sad mess of it'.[140] His was not a unique perspective. Press accounts make clear the public fascination with art spending, and the acquisitiveness of Morgan and Huntington was generally celebrated: wealthy Americans consolidating art treasures in the same manner they consolidated industries, remaking English libraries into collections that showcased only the finest, rarest, and most expensive books imaginable. Even the *Burlington Magazine* used the standard rhetoric of praise:

> Mr. Morgan was above everything a man of action. His successful raids upon the private collections of Europe were organized and carried out with the rapid decisive energy of a great general. He believed in military methods; he regarded rapidity and irrevocability of decision as more important than accuracy of judgment; he considered discipline more effective than a nice discrimination.[141]

However, Mencken took a very different view, believing that American collectors were motivated by 'the childish satisfaction of grabbing it and hoarding it'.[142]

---

[138] Ibid., 254.

[139] 'Mr. John Pierpont Morgan', *The Burlington Magazine*, 23(122), May 1913, p. 66.

[140] Rosenbach, *Books and Bidders*, p. 254.   [141] 'Mr. John Pierpont Morgan', p. 65.

[142] Mencken and Nathan, 'Clinical Notes', p. 57.

Overall, collectors benefited from this nationalistic narrative as it offered clear reasons for Americans to buy England's books. Throughout the period newspaper articles suggested that Europe was unwilling or unable to adequately preserve its own historical monuments. One example was Sulgrave Manor, the ancestral home of George Washington in Northamptonshire. In 1902 *The New York Times* reported that, 'lack of proper attention has already caused serious damage to some of the most interesting Washington reminiscences in Sulgrave [...] giving the house an aged appearance, which is decidedly more dilapidated than picturesque'.[143] The state of Sulgrave was also of interest to the American Scenic and Historic Preservation Society, an influential organisation whose annual reports monitored the condition of historic properties in America and, to a lesser extent, Britain. Morgan was at one point the honorary president and trustee of this organisation. Amongst American collectors stories circulated about valuable books housed in horrendous English conditions – often at the verge of destruction – before being discovered and rescued. Rosenbach shared two such stories with the *Saturday Evening Post*. In 1867 a copy of Shakespeare's 1599 *Venus and Adonis* was found in Lamport Hall in an old lumber room, where amongst 'piles of wood and discarded furniture he [London bookdealer Charles Edmunds] beheld stacks and stacks of dust-covered books. There were hundreds of them of various sizes and dates; some were chewed to bits, having furnished banquets for generations of mice'.[144] The book was eventually sold in 1919 for £15,100.[145] Huntington was the ultimate purchaser. A second copy of *Venus* was discovered shortly afterwards, when two young Englishmen were placing an old book in the branches of a tree for target practice. About to shoot arrows at the book, one of the young men considered the fact that the object might be valuable. He was right. That book was ultimately sold to Folger through Quaritch for £10,000/$50,000.[146] Along similar lines, Beverly Chew began the 'Foreword' to the Hoe Sale Catalogue with this anecdote:

---

[143] 'Vandalism at Sulgrave Manor', *NYT*, 14 September 1902, p. 25.

[144] Rosenbach, *Books and Bidders*, p. 51.   [145] Herrmann, *Sotheby's*, p. 200.

[146] 'News in Brief', *The Daily News*, 24 March 1920, p. 7; Rosenbach, *Books and Bidders*, p. 53.

> Mr. Hoe once told me, on his return to Europe, of a visit he
> had made to one of the great Libraries, and of his feelings of
> surprise and disgust at the utter lack of reverence and
> appreciation he found as shown in the want of care given
> [. . .] volume after volume was brought to him covered in
> dust, with leaves stained and bindings broken and in every
> way proclaiming the effects of indifference and neglect.[147]

Hoe replied: 'This confirms me in the conviction that those who love books
should have them in custody and will take the best care of them'. Chew
singled out English literature, stating that Hoe 'was always eager for
English literature and spared neither time nor money in a tireless quest
for the original editions of the authors who made our language great'.
Adding that, 'it may well be a cause for regret that many of its treasures may
find their way back to the old countries from which he brought them'.
Whipple agreed that his concerns were well-founded, telling *The New York
Times* in 1911: 'After seeing the generally careless way in which rare books
are housed in public libraries, especially in Europe, I fully share Mr. Hoe's
opinion that they are much better protected by private owners'.[148] The press
helped foster an image of American collectors as guardians of the national
textual heritage.

In contrast to popular depictions of English conditions, newspapers
often noted the remarkable state of preservation of rare books in
American libraries and the exhaustive efforts made to keep them safe. In
1906 the *Wall Street Journal* declared the new Morgan Library building: 'the
most perfect example of architecture in this country. It is intended to be
a treasure house', adding that, 'no other building in Europe or America was
ever erected with this care'.[149] Within these fabulous libraries, books were
housed in steel, guarded constantly, protected against every kind of threat –
human or natural. Some of the rare books in the new purpose-built

---

[147] B. Chew, 'Foreword', in *Catalogue of the Library of Robert Hoe of New York*
(New York: D. Taylor, 1911), p. v.

[148] '"Absurd" Prices', p. 10.

[149] 'J. Pierpont Morgan's New Library', *The Wall Street Journal*, 23 June 1906, p. 6.

Huntington Library were 'being better cared for than they ever were before', resting on, 'racks of steel', in conditions where, 'all natural light is excluded, and temperature and humidity are regulated carefully'.[150] A 1930 *Huntington Library Exhibition Catalogue* even told visitors precisely where to stand outside the building to see the entrance to the vault. Similarly, descriptions of the Morgan Library mentioned that manuscripts were kept in a room that was, 'a safe, burglar-proof and fire-proof. One enters by a thick steel door fitted with a combination lock, and the walls of the room are of steel, while a steel shutter protects the window at night'.[151] When Folger's collection was transported to Washington D.C., a *New York Times* headline read: 'Folger Books Moved by Armored Truck; Five Guards Take First Lot of $4,265,000 Shakespeareana to New Capital Library'.[152] When the paper introduced readers to the new Folger Library, it noted: 'Beneath and around all these Elizabethan properties are the efficient devices of a more modern age – vast steel vaults with intricate combinations, where the most valuable books and manuscripts will be locked away'.[153] And when John Pierpont Morgan Jr opened the Morgan Library to the public in 1924, he stated that his main priority was to make the rare books, 'permanently valuable', reminding reporters how fragile these items were, and how vulnerable in the wrong hands: 'one soiled thumb could undo the work of nine hundred years and a misplaced cough would be a disaster'.[154] This focus on the materiality of books, on books as fragile and acutely destructible objects, placed greater emphasis on the role of the collector as custodian of textual and material history. It also enabled American libraries to become emblematic of a national readiness to consolidate and safeguard threatened cultural artefacts. Yet to Mencken these

---

[150] M. E. Johnson, 'The Henry E. Huntington Library', *The English Journal*, 21(7) (September 1932), p. 530.

[151] 'Leading Collector of the Art World', p. 5.

[152] 'Folger Books Moved by Armored Truck', *NYT*, 21 October 1931, p. 19.

[153] E. F. Barnard, 'Shakespeare's Fane [*sic*] in the New World', *NYT*, 4 October 1931, p. 82.

[154] 'Puts Its Value at $8,500,000', *NYT*, 17 February 1924, p. 14.

actions were those of 'profiteers' hoarding their loot, creating 'vaults full of sunbursts', rather than true libraries.

Despite Mencken's scepticism, collectors could have deeply senti-mental, emotional attachments to their books. New York lawyer and collector Adrian Joline referred to his books as his 'pets', stating that, 'I look upon them almost as one might upon the children whom he must leave behind him [. . .] Some one will preserve them, and perhaps may fondle them as I have done'.[155] When collector Harry B. Smith sold his library in 1914 he wrote: 'The collecting of books is inspired by a sentiment founded on reverence and hero-worship'.[156] This was especially true of association copies or books with direct, personal ties to famous authors or former owners. Bibliographer Luther S. Livingston explained in 1914 that,

> We value these 'association' books because they bring us, [. . .] into direct communication with the writers. Our hands touch the same covers, our fingers touch the same leaves, our eyes look upon the same printed words [. . .] In the inscriptions in the books and in the manuscripts and auto-graph letters the great minds of the past come back again.[157]

Rosenbach told the *Saturday Evening Post* something similar, underscoring the power of an imagined relationship: 'To think that John Keats may have held in his slender white fingers your first edition of his poems; that his luminous eyes [. . .] may have lingered over the very pages of the copy you possess – this is enough to thrill the Devil himself!'.[158] Brayton Ives also wrote about a strongly emotive relationship with his books declaring: 'They

[155] A. H. Joline, *Meditations of an Autograph Collector* (New York: Harper & Brothers, 1902), p. 306.

[156] H. B. Smith, *A Sentimental Library: Comprising Books Formerly Owned by Famous Writers, Presentation Copies, Manuscripts, and Drawings Collected and Described by Harry B. Smith* (New York: De Vinne Press, 1914), p. xiv.

[157] L. S. Livingston, 'An Appreciation', in *A Sentimental Library*, pp. xvii–xviii.

[158] Rosenbach, *Books and Bidders*, p. 39.

have comforted me after many a weary day, and have stood often in the place of friends. I can hope nothing better for them and for their future owners than that they may receive as watchful care and give as much pleasure as while in my possession'.[159]

Perhaps in light of how he interacted with his books, Ives made clear the distinction that he possessed, 'only a Collection', and not a library at all – a statement which aligns with one of Mencken's accusations, albeit for entirely different reasons.[160] Harry B. Smith also made the claim that his library was not really a library in the traditional sense: 'There are millions of books fit only to read, but there are a few that should be treasured as the relics of the saints'.[161] In the case of Folger, there could be almost magical, transformative properties in the bibliographical features of certain volumes. He revealed as much in an essay about the Vincent First Folio of Shakespeare's works, a presentation copy that Folger called, 'the most precious book in the world'.[162] In 1907 Folger wrote an article on his Folio for *The Outlook*, stating that what made the book remarkable in bibliographical terms was 'trifling in the presence of this history of the book's genesis'.[163] Yet the bibliographical features of the volume, the material signs of its progress through early modern England – rather than the textual content alone – had the ability to transport modern witnesses to the seventeenth century: 'to the splendors and struggles of the reign of Elizabeth and James, when poets sang a glorious note, full-throated, when felonies were punished by branding the hand that stole, and ears were shorn to discourage eavesdropping where royalty conferred'.[164] However, far more public attention was paid to how Folger came to own his books. Even *The New York Times* refused to protest against Folger being labelled a 'reprehensible American millionaire', after he

[159] B. Ives, *Catalogue of the Collection of Books and Manuscripts Belonging to Mr. Brayton Ives of New-York* (New York: De Vinne Press, 1891), p. 5.

[160] Ibid., 1. [161] Smith, *Sentimental Library*, p. xii.

[162] H. C. Folger Jr., 'A Unique First Folio', *The Outlook*, 23 November 1907, p. 691; now Folger Library, Folger First Folio 1.

[163] Folger, 'Unique First Folio', p. 690. [164] Ibid., 691.

attempted to out-bid and out-manoeuvre Oxford's Bodleian Library for the Turbutt Folio in 1905.[165]

Mencken condemned actions like Folger's over the Turbutt Folio. However, within the collecting world, there was a broad range of responses to market developments which Mencken either overlooked or was unaware of. Some members of the book world argued that the strong market was not the result of individual actors, but was merely coincidental, a matter of good timing. In 1920, Cole stated that 'never, in the history of bookselling, has such a large number of superlatively rare books been offered for sale within such a limited period'.[166] Others focused on how a healthy book market brought greater attention to rare books, encouraging discoveries to be made (sometimes in old cupboards and attics) that otherwise would never take place. Some argued that book dealers, not collectors, were responsible for high prices.[167] Some that rising book prices were inevitable and not a product of reckless American spending. Following all the controversy surrounding the prices paid at the Hoe sale, after the final day of sales in 1911 the owner of the Anderson Auction Company, Major Emory S. Turner, made these closing remarks: 'there would come a time when the prices paid at this sale, instead of being thought "absurd," would be considered cheap; [. . .] This sale, he declared, would lead to a revision of values'.[168] Similarly, Whipple told *The New York Times*: 'I have read with much interest the criticisms of dealers and other buyers as to the "absurd" prices obtaining at the sale of Mr. Hoe's library. These critics forget that this is the dispersal of what for many years has been regarded as the finest private library in the world'.[169] Both were proved to be correct. Prices for remarkable rare books and manuscripts did keep rising, and the Hoe sale

---

[165] 'Topics of the Week', *NYT*, 31 March 1906, p. 26; R. M. Smith, 'Why a First Folio Shakespeare Remained in England', *The Review of English Studies*, 15(59) (1939), pp. 257–64.

[166] G. W. Cole, *Bibliography – A Forecast* (Chicago: University of Chicago Press, 1920), p. 1.

[167] G. E. Hale, 'The Huntington Library and Art Gallery', *Scribner's Magazine*, 82, 27 July 1927, p. 36.

[168] 'The Hoe Sale – III', *PW*, 13 May 1911, p. 2031.   [169] '"Absurd" Prices', p. 10.

would not be remembered for its absurdity. Instead, as a lasting reminder of its impact on the world of collecting – signalling the moment New York began to properly compete with London for dominance over the rare book market – from 1915 onwards, the famous Hoe sales figures would appear at the start of all Anderson catalogues.

Finally, some commentators emphasised how the feverish buying of American collectors like Morgan and Huntington aided scholarship. A *Scribner's Magazine* article published just after Huntington's death in 1927 stated that, thanks to Huntington: 'Manuscripts that have reposed in private coffers and books that have escaped the scholar in the safe retreat of country houses will soon serve for the production of new chapters in the history of literature, art, and science'.[170] While Mencken saw collecting as a source of Anglo-American tensions, this writer suggested that Huntington's collection, 'may serve to increase American appreciation of our debt to the past and aid in uniting the English-speaking peoples'.[171] He even argued that due to the 'heavy responsibility' of collecting, 'it can hardly be denied that Mr. Huntington has amply repaid his indebtedness to the rich resources of England'.[172] Finally, in a statement indicative of how many in the early-twentieth century defended the growth of American cultural institutions, he added, that the Library, 'offers one of the most effective means of studying the transfer of civilization to the New World'.[173] Thus in draining English libraries, many Americans convinced themselves that leading collectors were merely keeping the shared cultural treasures of two nations permanently valuable.

1.6 Conclusions

Press articles celebrating the acquisition of art objects bought at exceptionally high prices at spectacular sales gave the impression that America was draining England of its finite historical treasures at a rapid rate. Among the most visible participants in this activity were Morgan and Huntington, who spent fortunes on books. The value of the Morgan Library was estimated at $8,500,000 in 1924, and the Huntington library was estimated to have

[170] Hale, 'The Huntington Library', p. 43. [171] Ibid. [172] Ibid. [173] Ibid., 35.

already cost $10,000,000 by 1922.[174] Moreover, both men bought items that could justly be called English national treasures; housing them in lavish purpose-built spaces, publicly advertising the cultural significance of their holdings. Yet Mencken was only responding to one part – the most visible part – of a far more nuanced story. In reality, of course, early-twentieth-century American book collectors were remarkably varied in their personal strategies, motivations, and collecting goals. However, as Mencken illustrated, the American public was made far more aware of a cohesive, muscular narrative of rescue buying, one that celebrated American consumerism and methods of preservation. According to this narrative, national treasures were not being raided from England. Instead, books that had survived for centuries were at grave material risk, requiring American steel vaults rather than crumbling English private libraries to safeguard a collective Anglo-American identity.

---

[174] 'Puts Its Value at $8,500,000', p. 14; 'Rare Books, Autographs and Prints', *PW*, 15 April 1922, p. 1129.

2 British Perspectives

A cartoon by Bernard Partridge published in the British magazine *Punch* in 1922 depicts the fictional American Uncle Sam with a Shakespeare First Folio under one arm and Thomas Gainsborough's *The Blue Boy* under the other (Figure 2). The choice of items was inspired by purchases in London by the real Americans Henry Folger and Henry Huntington. In the cartoon Uncle Sam stands next to Shakespeare's grave with the nervous ghost of Shakespeare behind him. The caption reads 'Autolycus, U.S.A.', a reference to Autolycus the trickster and 'snapper-up of unconsidered trifles' in Shakespeare's *The Winter's Tale*, inspired in turn by Greek mythology.[175] Reading the famous inscription on Shakespeare's memorial that curses anyone who moves the bones, Uncle Sam declares 'Now, that's real disappointing. I'd set my heart on that skeleton'. The ghost of Shakespeare replies: 'But all the same I should feel more comfortable if it was insured'. The cartoon forms part of a long-running tradition of presenting Americans denuding Britain of her most precious cultural treasures, in a variety of forms, at almost any cost. However, it is unusual in hinting at trickery rather than simply the power of American money, in the presence of which concerns about British culture tended to become as insubstantial as Shakespeare's ghost. Indeed, Shakespeare's suggestion that his bones could be insured implies an acceptance that a financial value could be put on anything.

Despite frequent expressions of concern about the impact of American demand for rare books on the ability of British collectors and museums to secure items between 1890 and 1929, no measures were taken to control their exportation before the Second World War.[176] In practice, therefore, the wishes of British collectors and scholars took second place to those of British sellers. Limited government support for the acquisition of objects for museums and libraries

---

[175] W. Shakespeare, *The Winter's Tale*, IV.3.

[176] See A. N. L. Munby and L. W. Turner, *The Flow of Books and Manuscripts* (Los Angeles: William Andrews Clark Memorial Library, 1969), p. 10.

Figure 2 B. Partridge, 'Autolycus U.S.A.', *Punch*, 24 May 1922

prompted the creation of organisations including, in 1903, the National Art-Collections Fund (NACF), to try to address the perceived problem of the loss of British artistic treasures.[177] In addition, changes in the market for books, including, but not limited to, the increasing impact of a small number of very wealthy American buyers at sales in Britain, prompted shifts in attitudes towards 'America' over the course of the period. At the turn of the century concerns about American purchases of rare books were expressed publicly and privately, but went largely unheeded, in part because plenty of material was available. In the years around the First World War American dealers contributed to new auction records and ensured these were well-publicised, but reaction in the British press was relatively muted, reflecting changing social attitudes to elite collecting in Britain and the economic realities of funding a major war. By the end of the war the dominance of wealthy Americans was inescapable, but British sellers continued to benefit from high prices and commentators enjoyed the spectacle of record sales at auction, whilst British collectors found other ways to create libraries. Throughout, London remained a major trading centre for rare books, and American buyers were only part of a diverse market, albeit receiving a disproportionate amount of comment in the press.

2.1 The 'Drain'

On 7 July 1902 the London *Times* included an article written in response to J. P. Morgan's purchase (for £130,000) of the library of Richard Bennett, director of John Smith Jr. & Co., bleachers of calico from Lancashire.[178] The author asked:

---

[177] See R. C. Witt, 'A Movement in Aid of Our National Art Collections', *Nineteenth Century and After*, 54(320) (October 1903), pp. 651–9; 'The National Art-Collections Fund', *The Times*, 12 November 1903, p. 6; *Twenty-Five Years of the National Art-Collections Fund 1903–1928* (Glasgow: Glasgow University Press, 1928).

[178] For Morgan's purchase of the Bennett collection see: James, *Catalogue of Manuscripts*; Herrmann, *Sotheby's*, p. 120; P. Needham, 'William Morris's "Ancient Books" at Sale', in R. Myers, M. Harris, and G. Mandelbrote (eds.), *Under the Hammer: Book Auctions since the Seventeenth Century* (New Castle: Oak Knoll Press, 2001), pp. 183–4.

> Can nothing be done to stem the continuous and wholesale
> exportation of rare early printed and other books and illu-
> minated MSS. to the United States of America? The 'drain'
> has been going on for over half-a-century; within recent
> years it has reached huge proportions; and now we have the
> mournful privilege of chronicling the most important single
> transaction which has occurred – or, perhaps, is likely to
> occur – in connexion with this subject.[179]

The sale was deemed to be particularly significant because of its size (about
700 books) and its contents, which included illuminated manuscripts and
early printed books, among which were thirty-two Caxtons. Moreover, the
library contained some of the most expensive books from the library of the
socialist and designer William Morris, who had died in 1896. The author of
the article judged that 'The formation of another such collection scarcely
comes within the range of the possible – even granted half a century and an
unlimited amount of money to attempt such a task'. This was a remarkable
conclusion given that Morris had acquired most of his medieval manuscripts
in the last five years of his life, but it finds echoes in other concerns that the
abundant supply of rare books on the London market in the 1890s was
beginning to dry up.[180] In this the author's view was to prove overly
pessimistic, although the Bennett library was not to be the last major
collection to cross the Atlantic in a single purchase. In conclusion, the
Times' author bowed to American financial power, declaring: 'It is, [. . .]
little short of a public calamity for the collection to pass out of this country;
but, unfortunately, in these matters there is no such element as sentiment –
the man with the biggest purse gets the prize'. Yet, the article's final
sentence offered a glimmer of consolation: 'If English collectors will not
avail themselves of such unique opportunities, it is, at all events, comforting

---

[179] 'The Exportation of Rare Books to America', *The Times*, 7 July 1902, p. 14.

[180] See B. Quaritch, 'Note', in *A Catalogue of Ancient, Illuminated & Liturgical
Manuscripts* (London: Bernard Quaritch, 1902), p. v; on Morris' collection see:
P. Needham, 'William Morris: Book Collector', in P. Needham (ed.), *William
Morris and the Art of the Book* (Oxford: Oxford University Press, 1976), pp.
21–47; M. Braesel, *William Morris und die Buchmalerei* (Cologne: Böhlau, 2019).

to reflect that, [. . .] the collection is in the custody of an English-speaking nation'. The pain of geographical distance might be soothed by a notion of cultural influence associated with a shared language.

By 1902 the idea of Americans as a threat to British collections was well established. At the auction of Morris' library in 1898, held once Bennett (who had bought Morris' collection *en bloc* in 1897) had selected the items he would incorporate into his own collection, one reporter attributed high prices to 'the spirited bidding of the gentleman who is said to be buying for America'.[181] Yet although Americans were present, including Henry Wellcome, who had made a fortune from pharmaceuticals and was resident in London, and Benjamin Franklin Stevens, who exported books to America, the highest prices were actually paid by British-based collectors and dealers. Similarly, Bernard Quaritch held bids on behalf of Americans, but the results were modest. For example, John Boyd Thacher of Albany, New York obtained two lots for a total of £7 3s.[182] Spending on a larger scale, Robert Hoe bought two lots through Quaritch for £360 16s, but his outlay was eclipsed by that of the British collectors Laurence Hodson, whose bill from Quaritch for items bought at the Morris sale came to £1,069 19s, and Henry Yates Thompson (former owner of the *Pall Mall Gazette*), who paid the highest price for a single item: £350 for the Sherbrooke Missal, an early fourteenth-century manuscript made in East Anglia.[183] While Americans contributed to the bidding, therefore, there is no evidence that they significantly increased prices, let alone putting material out of reach of British buyers. At the same time, books from Morris' collection left Britain via Quaritch for other destinations, including Paris and Leipzig, without prompting any comment in the press.

Concerns about the departure of material from Britain led to the creation of the National Art-Collections Fund in 1903, 'to meet the severe and increasing competition of private collectors and public institutions, both

---

[181] 'Book and Curio Sales', *Glasgow Herald*, 10 December 1898, p. 7.

[182] London, Bernard Quaritch Ltd., Commission Book, 1895–99.

[183] Ibid.; the Sherbrooke Missal is now Aberystwyth, National Library of Wales, MS 15536E.

in Europe and America'.[184] At the time it was acknowledged that America's acquisitions were 'checked for the moment by the "slump" in America', though it was feared they were sure 'to begin again when speculators once more begin to make fortunes'.[185] In a reflection on the fund's activities written a quarter of a century later, the role of American collectors in driving up prices received particular emphasis:

> Above all the United States had definitely entered the lists to win all that was finest and rarest in the world of art. The building up of the great Pierpont Morgan Collection had begun, soon to be followed by those of Mr. S. Gardner [Mrs Isabella Stewart Gardner], Mr. Frick, Mr. Johnson, Mr. Widener and other great private collections as well as of public museums in New York, Boston, Philadelphia and elsewhere.[186]

Yet this account was written with the benefit of hindsight, and in 1903 books were not among the NACF's priorities. Having facilitated the donation of books and manuscripts, in 1920 the fund made its first contribution to the purchase of an illuminated manuscript: £1,000 towards the acquisition of the Life of Saint Cuthbert bought by the British Museum for £5,000.[187] At that auction the British Museum faced competition from Americans, as Quaritch's archives record that firm received commissions from Abraham Rosenbach and Henry Walters for the manuscript. Expecting that the book would sell for a high figure, Julius Gilson of the British Museum sought donations from British collectors as well as the NACF.[188] Because the book had been made in Durham he targeted people in the north of England, playing on the emotive power of connection to a particular place as an argument for its retention in Britain.[189] After the sale Gilson wrote an article

---

[184] 'The National Art-Collections Fund', p. 6.

[185] [untitled article], *The Times*, 12 November 1903, p. 7.

[186] *Twenty-Five Years of the National Art-Collections Fund*, p. 4.

[187] Now British Library, Yates Thompson, MS 26.

[188] Tate Archive, TGA 9328, National Art-Collections Fund, Acquisition File 292.

[189] Ibid.; *National Art-Collections Fund Seventeenth Annual Report* (London: NACF, 1920), p. 28.

for *The Observer* in which he argued that the British 'must resign ourselves
to see many of our treasures pass away from Europe to countries where as
yet there is not a fine Psalter or Book of Hours in a thousand square miles.
And we can afford to do so'.[190] However, he claimed that 'there are a few
manuscripts still in private hands which for one reason or another are
national monuments and should not be allowed to leave the country'.
Gilson saw the NACF as playing a valuable role in this context, encouraging vendors to work with the fund 'and other agencies' to keep the works
in Britain, rather than seeking hasty sales.

In the NACF's 1928 publication the Director and Principal Librarian of the
British Museum, Frederic Kenyon, stressed what he described as the 'insuffi-
ciently realized' importance of 'English painting' in the period *c.* 700–1400,
much of which was preserved in books.[191] A similar case was made in 1932,
when the NACF contributed to the purchase of the de Brailes leaves for £3,500
for the Fitzwilliam Museum in Cambridge. This set of six illuminated leaves
had been part of a manuscript made in Oxford in the thirteenth century. The
illumination was identified as the work of William de Brailes by the director of
the Fitzwilliam, Sydney Cockerell, on a visit to Rosenbach's New York shop in
1920.[192] The leaves had not been in America for very long, having been part of
the auction of the Earl of Ashburnham's collection in London in 1901, when
they were bought by Quaritch for £390. At that time the British Museum had
been prepared to spend £200 on them, and the Fitzwilliam Museum just £30.[193]
In 1920 Cockerell was in America with (and funded by) the American Alfred
Chester Beatty, who bought the leaves for $6,000 (£1,200) and took them back
to London. (Having made a fortune as a mining engineer in America, from
1913 Beatty divided his time between London and the USA).[194] In 1932 the

---

[190] J. P. Gilson, 'Illuminated Manuscripts', *The Observer*, 28 March 1920, p. 8.

[191] F. Kenyon, 'Manuscripts', in *Twenty-Five Years of the National Art-Collections
       Fund*, pp. 200–1.

[192] S. C. Cockerell, 'Diary 1920', British Library, Add. MS 52657, f. 53v.

[193] London, Bernard Quaritch Ltd., Commission Book, 1899–1903.

[194] On Beatty see: L. Cleaver, 'The Western Manuscript Collection of Alfred
       Chester Beatty (ca. 1915–1930)', *Manuscript Studies*, 2(2) (2017), 445–82, with
       further bibliography.

Times deemed the de Brailes leaves' acquisition for the Fitzwilliam 'poetic justice', declaring that 'But for the action of the National Art-Collections Fund these masterpieces of early English art would almost certainly have returned to America' when Beatty's collection was put up for sale that year.[195]

Manuscripts did not have to be either British-made or long-term residents in British libraries for the threat of American collectors to be invoked. In addition to the de Brailes leaves, in 1904 Cockerell attempted to interest Henry Guppy of the Rylands Library in Manchester in manuscripts owned by the artist and dealer Charles Fairfax Murray, including a fifteenth-century manuscript in French and made in France, and a thirteenth-century English Apocalypse (both probably bought by Murray in Paris), on the grounds that 'I don't want these treasures to go to America'.[196] Guppy did not buy the collection, but they did not immediately find an American buyer, and instead were bought in 1905–6 by the British collector Charles Dyson Perrins.[197] (The Apocalypse went to America after the sale of the Perrins collection in 1959, the French manuscript is now in Berlin.)[198]

Rather more plausibly, in 1918, following Yates Thompson's announcement of his intention to sell his collection, Perrins expressed concern that 'your volumes will go to swell the Morgan collection in New York', a view shared by Cockerell, although Morgan's librarian, Belle Greene declined an offer to negotiate for the entire collection.[199] Instead at the first sale of twenty-eight manuscripts and two early printed books from Yates

---

[195] 'The "Brailes Leaves"', *The Times*, 21 May 1932, p. 8.

[196] Manchester, John Rylands Library Archive, JRL/4/1/1904/121.

[197] See L. Cleaver, 'Charles William Dyson Perrins as a Collector of Medieval and Renaissance Manuscripts c. 1900–1920', *Perspectives médiévales*, 41 (2020), http://journals.openedition.org/peme/19776.

[198] The manuscripts are now Los Angeles, J. Paul Getty Museum MS Ludwig III. 1 and Berlin, Staatsbibliothek Preussischer Kulturbesitz, HS 94.

[199] University of Birmingham, Cadbury Research Library, Ladd/4570. Letter from C. W. Dyson Perrins to H. Yates Thompson, 19 November 1918; S. C. Cockerell, 'Diary 1919', British Library Add. MS 52656, f. 25v, entry for 4 June 1919; New York, Morgan Library Archive, ARC 1310 MCC Quaritch VII, annotated telegram dated 30 August 1918; see also Herrmann, *Sotheby's*, pp. 187–9.

Thompson's collection in 1919, the Morgan Library obtained five items for a total of £9,950 (19 per cent of the proceeds of the sale).[200] George D. Smith bought a collection of maps for Huntington, but other purchases were destined for Baron Édmond de Rothschild and Callouste Gulbenkian, both of whom were based in Paris. All was not lost for Britain, however, as the British Museum acquired a fourteenth-century French illuminated manuscript (now British Library Yates Thompson MS 11) for £4,200 and a fifteenth-century Florentine printed book for £500, apparently outbidding at least one American for the former.[201] In addition, the Briton Thomas Riches bought four volumes, including one for the Fitzwilliam Museum, to which he and his wife later bequeathed the rest, and another British collector, William Harrison Woodward, secured one manuscript.[202] At the second Yates Thompson sale in 1920 American buyers obtained a similar percentage of the books on offer. This time the auction included twenty-six manuscripts and eight printed books. According to Sotheby's annotated catalogue, the New York dealer Lathrop C. Harper bought a thirteenth-century manuscript from Waltham Abbey, and Quaritch held bids from American clients.[203] The firm obtained twenty of the thirty-four books, of which two were destined for Walters, one for Morgan, and three for the New York Public

---

[200] The manuscripts are now New York, Morgan Library, M.639, M.641, M.642, M.644.

[201] For Widener's interest see New York, Morgan Library Archive, ARC 1310 MCC Quaritch VII, letter from E. H. Dring to B. Greene, 11 June 1919.

[202] For Riches see 'Mr. T. H. Riches', *The Times*, 21 September 1935, p. 12; F. Wormald and P. M. Giles, 'A Handlist of the Additional Manuscripts in the Fitzwilliam Museum, Part III', *Transactions of the Cambridge Bibliographical Society*, 1(5) (1953), pp. 365–75; S. Panayotova, 'Cockerell and Riches', in J. H. Marrow, R. A. Linenthal, and W. Noel (eds.), *The Medieval Book: Glosses from Friends & Colleagues of Christopher de Hamel* ('t Goy-Houten: Hes & De Graaf, 2010), pp. 377–86. The manuscript bought by Woodward is now Cologny, Fondation Martin Bodmer, Cod. Bodmer 78.

[203] London, Bernard Quaritch Ltd., Commission Book, 1917–20. The manuscript bought by Harper is now Princeton University Library, Garrett MS 114.

Library.[204] Quaritch also secured two volumes for Perrins, one for the British Museum, and five for Beatty. Again, America was not the sole destination for books or driver of high prices, as Gulbenkian spent significantly more on four books (£21,400) than the seven books destined for America (which came to a total of £12,550). By 1920, therefore, the 'drain' lamented in 1902 was significant, though supply in Britain was hardly running dry.

2.2 The 'Zest'

By the time of the First World War there could be no doubt that Americans were obtaining desirable books in large quantities from Britain. In addition to auctions, Smith bought parts of the library of the Dukes of Devonshire in 1914, followed by the Bridgewater Library in 1917.[205] Although this was a matter of concern among some British collectors and scholars, no laws were passed to prevent material from being exported.[206] Moreover, occasional voices were raised in defence of American contributions to the trade. In 1917 an article by Clement King Shorter, himself a collector, declared:

> I have no sympathy with the occasional outcry when our valuable books or art treasures go to America. If they are to be shut up in private houses they may as well rejoice the heart of an American magnate as of an English magnate. Only when they are purchased by the nation is there subject for rejoicing, and our nation is not likely to purchase art or literary treasures for a long time to come. So far from the American collector doing us any harm, he actually adds a zest to book-collecting,[207]

---

[204] These are now: Baltimore, Walters Art Museum, W.34, W.125–6; New York, Morgan Library, M.970; New York Public Library, MSS Spencer 2, Spencer 3.
[205] Dickinson, 'Mr. Huntington and Mr. Smith', 377, 387–8; see also Section 1.3.
[206] Munby and Tower, *Flow of Books and Manuscripts*, p. 8.
[207] C. K. S[horter], 'A Literary Letter: Millionaires as Book Collectors', *The Sphere*, 2 June 1917, p. 198.

The 'zest' was presumably the excitement generated by new auction records, which was coupled with the investment of large sums of money at a time when Britain's resources were being drained by war.

The sale of the first part of the Hoe library in 1911 had provided a very public demonstration of American financial dominance. European dealers went to New York for the event, including Alfred Quaritch, who wrote to the Parisian bookseller Édouard Rahir, 'I hope that the books will not sell high, so that in future they may send their libraries to Europe for sale'.[208] It was not to be. At the end of the first sale Belle Greene expressed her frustration at the disruption of the old order. She claimed 'Buyers have come from all over Europe and are getting nothing', showing public sympathy and even allyship with the Europeans.[209] In fact, the European dealers did not come away empty-handed, the New York *Sun* reporting that 'Although George D. Smith continued to take a majority of the offerings, Bernard Quaritch insisted on having a share of the best lots'.[210] However, there was no question of the rest of the sales being held in London. Moreover, Quaritch's clients at the Hoe sale included William A. White and the Morgan Library, so a purchase by the London-based dealer did not necessarily mean that the books were destined for Europe.

The first Hoe sale was a major event, in part because auctions of large collections of rare books were still relatively uncommon in America. Yet Britain was not short of large sales. In 1911, as the first Hoe sale was in preparation, it was announced that in London Sotheby's would sell the enormous collection created by Henry Huth and his son Alfred Henry. The latter's will included an unusual clause that stated that if his library was to be sold, before the auction the Trustees of the British Museum were to select fifty books for the museum. Those books were to be marked 'Huth bequest' and a catalogue issued. Huth gave no reason for this decision, but in the resulting catalogue Kenyon observed that it 'allowed the national collection to acquire exactly those books which to it were of the greatest importance, and which it could not hope to be able to acquire in competition at public

---

[208] London, Bernard Quaritch Ltd., Hoe Sale Letters, letter from B. A. Quaritch to É. Rahir, 6 April 1911.

[209] 'J. P. Morgan's Librarian Says High Book Prices are Harmful', p. 13.

[210] '$42,800 for "Morte d'Arthur"', *The New York Sun*, 2 May 1911, p. 1.

auction'.[211] The Trustees selected thirty-seven printed books, including a Caxton and three Shakespeare Quartos, and thirteen manuscripts. In both categories the material was not restricted to books made in Britain. Of the manuscripts, Kenyon commented 'Since the British Museum already possesses by far the finest collection of English illuminated manuscripts in existence, this preponderance of foreign examples [in the Huth Library] is entirely to its advantage'.[212] Moreover, as Alfred Pollard noted, Huth's will was particularly advantageous to the museum in that it allowed it to obtain, 'all the first-class books which it really needed out of his collection, with a considerable number of those on the borderland of the class, while leaving it to buy from its own resources such of the less valuable books as it desired'.[213] Pollard noted that at the first Huth sale the museum obtained twenty-eight books, mostly English, but Quaritch's records reveal that the museum was outbid on two manuscripts: lot 538 (a fifteenth-century prayer roll) and lot 648, an 'Anglo-Norman' Bible, as well as a further twenty-two printed books. Similarly, at the third sale in 1913, the British Museum obtained twenty-seven printed books but lost out on thirty others and one manuscript. For the 1913 Huth sale Quaritch received commissions from overseas clients in Maryland, Massachusetts, New York, Ohio, and Pennsylvania, as well as France, Germany, Morocco, the Netherlands, Russia, Spain, Sweden, and New Zealand.[214] However, Huntington's commissions for that sale filled eleven pages of Quaritch's commission book, eclipsing all other buyers, and he obtained almost everything he wanted.

In the summer of 1914, Smith came to London once again prepared to spend large sums. In July the New York *Sun* reported that he had spent $494,380 (about £100,000) in a few weeks.[215] Smith also staged an exhibition in Selfridge's department store. *The Illustrated London News* commented:

> If the strength and danger of the American collector is still
> but vaguely apprehended, a visit to the exhibition in Oxford

[211] *Catalogue of the Fifty Manuscripts & Printed Books Bequeathed to the British Museum by Alfred H. Huth* (London: British Museum, 1912), p. v.

[212] Ibid., vi.   [213] Ibid., xiii.

[214] London, Bernard Quaritch Ltd., Commission Book, 1913–17.

[215] 'American Smashes London Book Ring', *The New York Sun*, 18 July 1914, p. 1.

Street of books belonging to Mr. George D. Smith of New York will serve as an illustration. The true patriot can thereby suffer the exquisite humiliation of seeing in Selfridge's Palm Court [...] Caxtons that are not in the British Museum, and other books [...] from the Pembroke Library, the Chatsworth Library, the Hoe Library, and with most of the good things from the Huth Library.[216]

In addition to his purchases, Smith was driving up prices for some books. On 9 July 1914, at the sale of another part of the Huth Library, he was the underbidder for a quarto of *King Lear* published in 1604, which was sold to Quaritch for Folger for £2,470. The *Pall Mall Gazette* reported that this 'more than quadruples the record at Sotheby's for a quarto play, and exceeds all but the highest sums ever paid for a First Folio of Shakespeare'.[217] Quaritch's records reveal that another of his American clients, White, had been prepared to pay just £460, and the firm had no commissions for the book from British buyers. Record prices were good for dealers (although Quaritch charged Folger just 5 per cent commission on the sale) and they increased the potential value of collections, but British collectors were finding themselves increasingly priced out of the market. At the 1914 Huth sale, the British Museum obtained just three of the thirteen items it wanted, for a total of £153 10s. The museum did not bid for the quarto, perhaps anticipating that it would be unaffordable.

In addition to the drama created by Smith's high prices, some Americans brought glamour to London's auction rooms. In 1920, *The Sketch* reported that 'Miss Belle Green [*sic*], the librarian of the Morgan Library was the only very American person at the Sotheby sale of Yates Thompson manuscripts', describing her as 'Very American, and very nice-looking, in a hat of red feathers'.[218] While the comment could be read as a hint at Greene's African-American heritage, it probably simply reflects an idea of American glamour.

---

[216] E. M., 'Art Notes', *The Illustrated London News*, 18 July 1914, p. 108.

[217] '£2,470 for "King Leir": Record Price at Huth Library Sale', *Pall Mall Gazette*, 9 July 1914, p. 2.

[218] 'Look Here', *The Sketch*, 31 March 1920, p. 489; see also C. K. S[horter], 'A Literary Letter: The R. L. Stevenson Club', *The Sphere*, 10 April 1920, p. 48.

Greene stood out, in part, as a woman in the auction room, though she was not the only woman to attend sales. However, whilst men's appearance received less comment, the activities of American dealers appeared in magazines like *The Tatler*, which in 1924 reported that Rosenbach had bought most of the books of the Britwell Court Library and had come to Europe 'quite prepared to spend between £300,000 and £400,000'. The author pondered, 'Would it be possible, I wonder, for some statistician to calculate precisely how long it will be before all the treasures of Europe have found their way over to America?'[219]

Yet collectors in Britain did not have to build their libraries through auctions. They could, if they wished, visit dealers' shops on a regular basis and had easier access to Europe. This was not necessarily better value, but it allowed for deliberation and negotiation. In the 1890s Morris had the Huntingfield Psalter 'on approval' from Quaritch while he agonised over the price, and he obtained a discount of £50 from Jacques Rosenthal of Munich for a Book of Hours.[220] In 1919, Beatty's wife Edith persuaded Yates Thompson to sell her a richly decorated fifteenth-century manuscript Book of Hours privately for £4,000.[221] The following year Beatty visited the substantial remains of the library of Sir Thomas Phillipps at Cheltenham and over the next five years he and Edith made private purchases from Phillipps' grandson, Thomas Fitzroy Fenwick. In December 1920 Beatty bought twenty-four manuscripts from Fenwick for £11,954.[222] The price was negotiated, but for both Beatty and Fenwick it removed the risk of an auction and the added costs of auction house and dealers' fees.

When Smith bought the Bridgewater collection *en bloc* in 1917, as with Morgan's purchase of the Bennett collection, the buyer was initially kept anonymous. However, it was soon reported that the library had been

---

[219] 'The Letters of Evelyn', p. 93.

[220] N. Kelvin (ed.), *The Collected Letters of William Morris*, 4 vols. (Princeton: Princeton University Press, 1984–96), IV, pp. 180–2, 299.

[221] Cockerell, 'Diary 1919', f. 23; Cleaver, 'Western Manuscript Collection', 458.

[222] Oxford, Bodleian Library, MS Phillipps-Robinson c. 719, letter dated 17 December 1920; Munby, *Dispersal*, pp. 71–5.

acquired by Smith 'at a price stated to be over £200,000'.[223] The sale was noted in the British press with little protest. *The Guardian* declared that 'There is reason to fear that the famous Ellesmere Library [. . .] has gone the way of so many precious English books and pictures – across the Atlantic'.[224] However, as *The Tatler* (founded by Shorter) put it: 'it's rather awful isn't it? – that the glorious Bridgewater Library should have had to go to America, but as the new owner – who's that greatest of book collectors, the billionaire Henry E. Huntington – is said to have paid Lord Ellesmere over £200,000 for it, well ... After all, money *talks*, and books don't say a word, out loud'.[225] This combination of hand-wringing and resignation set the tone for British attitudes in the following decade.

2.3 Money Talks

Money continued to talk as the trade in rare books boomed at the end of the First World War and into the 1920s. Although some dealers had tried to maintain 'business as usual' on the outbreak of war, most London auctions were suspended in the autumn of 1914.[226] However, when it became clear that the war was not going to be over by Christmas, sales in aid of the Red Cross helped to make buying luxury goods socially acceptable again and international trade gradually resumed. By the end of the war American dominance at the top of the market was widely assumed. In 1919, Belle Greene wrote to Edmund Dring, who had taken over running Quaritch's business after Alfred's death in 1913, about the first Yates Thompson sale. She asked, 'Is there any collector of importance, at the present time, in England, except Mr. Dyson Perrins?'[227] That 'importance' meant the ability to spend large sums was recognised in Dring's response, which declared that Perrins was:

[223] 'The Bridgwater Library', *The Times*, 19 May 1917, p. 9.

[224] 'The Ellesmere Library', *The Manchester Guardian*, 18 May 1917, p. 4.

[225] 'The Letters of Eve', *The Tatler*, 30 May 1917, p. 262; for Shorter's involvement see C. K. Shorter, *C. K. S. An Autobiography: A Fragment by Himself*, ed. J. M. Bulloch (London: privately printed, 1927), p. 102.

[226] 'Bookworms in War', *The Times*, 4 January 1916, p. 11.

[227] New York, Morgan Library Archive, ARC 1310 MCC Quaritch VII, letter from B. Greene to E. H. Dring, 21 April 1919.

the only man who would spend £15000 or £20000 at a sale,
but on the other hand there are at least half a dozen people
who would be quite willing to buy one fine manuscript at
a cost of say two or three thousand pounds just for the sake
of possessing one really good specimen of early art, and that
will be my difficulty in regard to the sale.[228]

Dring was probably overstating the figures, and Perrins had already
indicated doubts about participating in the sale, declaring 'I am a little
afraid they will go beyond what I would feel justified in giving in times like
these'.[229] However, among the collectors in Dring's mind may have been
Riches, Charles St John Hornby, and Beatty. The latter had started to spend
large sums on manuscripts, for example, purchasing the de Levis Hours,
which Quaritch had acquired at the Hoe sale in 1912 for $6,500 (£1,300), in
1916 for £2,000.[230] After the sale Dring reported to Greene, 'I was rather
surprised to get Lot 30 [an Aristotle printed in 1483] for £2,900, as I quite
expected that G.D.S. [Smith] would have sent a very long commission for
such an important book. The underbidder was B. F. Stevens who was
bidding undoubtedly for an American client who I rather think lives in
New York'.[231] Although Americans only bought a minority of the lots at
that sale, therefore, a small number of Americans were contributing to
a boom in the market for certain kinds of rare books and manuscripts.

Following Smith's sudden death in March 1920, Rosenbach assumed his
roles buying books for Huntington and fuelling reports about American
successes in the American press. In April 1921, under the headline
'ROSENBACH BRINGS FORTUNE IN BOOKS' *The New York Times*
reported that Rosenbach had spent $1,000,000 in London. The article noted
that Rosenbach had paid £41,000 at the Britwell sale, which it described as

[228] Ibid., letter from E. H. Dring to B. Greene, 8 May 1919.
[229] London, Bernard Quaritch Ltd., letter from C. W. Dyson Perrins to
E. H. Dring, 15 April 1919.
[230] Cleaver, 'Western Manuscript Collection', 479, no. lx; now New Haven,
Beinecke Library, MS 400.
[231] New York, Morgan Library Archive, ARC 1310 MCC Quaritch VII, letter from
E. H. Dring to B. Greene, 11 June 1919.

'another example, of which the late George D. Smith furnished so many to the English collecting world, of the eagerness in this country for the choicest treasures in bibliography and the willingness to pay for them'.[232] This kind of comment prompted Henry Mencken's reaction in *The American Mercury* in 1925, in which he suggested that behind the famous English good manners, the British detested American collectors.[233]

Yet, while British commentators in the 1920s continued to express frustration at the departure of books, at least one English reader of *The American Mercury* disagreed.[234] Writing in *The Sphere*, Shorter claimed firstly that 'A great many of the books sold to America come back to England'.[235] Some books did return, including the de Brailes leaves, though the phrase 'a great many' was probably overstating the case. Secondly, and more plausibly, the author declared 'A great many of the books sold in England do really get into English libraries'. Indeed in 1920 another commentator had observed in the context of Rosenbach's purchase of the Stowe papers for Huntington, that even if Britain could buy such things where to store them would pose a problem as 'The Public Record Office is getting too small, even for our state documents'.[236] Finally, however, ignoring the case made by Mencken that most students of rare English books lived in Britain, Shorter sided (once again) with the British sellers. He declared:

> My own feeling with regard to book-collecting is that we are
> one people, and I do not much mind whether a book is in
> California or is in Middlesex. I am just as likely ever to see it
> at Pasadena as I am in Bloomsbury. In fact, I have been in
> Pasadena within the last ten years, and I have not been in the
> British Museum during that period.

Ignoring the views of those who *did* frequent the British Museum, he continued, 'So far as Americans have raised the price of rare books, I am rather pleased. Now and again they have put a little money into my pocket'.

[232] 'Rosenbach Brings Fortune in Books', *NYT*, 26 April 1921, p. 14.

[233] Mencken and Nathan, 'Clinical Notes', pp. 56–7; see also Section 1.1.

[234] A further example of British frustration is: 'Acquisitive America', *Westminster Gazette*, 18 May 1922, p. 6.

[235] S[horter], 'A Literary Letter: The Solidarity of Book-Collecting', p. 38.

[236] 'The Way of the World', *The Graphic*, 20 February 1920, p. 324.

Yet while some commentators were happy for books in private hands to leave the country, the departure of books from institutional collections was more controversial. Even Shorter expressed qualms at the sale of the Royal Society's books in 1925. Shorter celebrated his friend Rosenbach's success, but added 'It is a nice point whether the Royal Society should have sold [. . .], however hard up it may be for the latest scientific instruments'.[237] He continued:

> What is wanted in this country is the spirit which has actuated Pierpont Morgan and Huntington in America. We desire to see rich men collect libraries and give them to public institutions. What encouragement will they have to do this? What finality will they see even in a great university or museum when so glamorous a body as the Royal Society will stoop to the auction-room.

A variation on this problem occurred in 1929. Two illuminated manuscripts, the fourteenth-century Luttrell Psalter, which had been on loan to the British Museum since 1909, and the fifteenth-century Bedford Psalter-Hours, recently deposited at the museum, were to be sold by the owner who had inherited them.[238] The museum staff wanted to acquire the books but knew that they were unlikely to be able to afford them at auction. Recognising that American collectors would be interested, Eric Millar, who worked at the museum and was also creating a catalogue of Beatty's western manuscripts, wrote to Greene: 'we should be enormously grateful to Mr Morgan if he would resist any private offer of the books, and if you could help us by giving Dr Rosenbach and any others who may occur to

[237] C. K. S[horter], 'A Literary Letter: The Ideal Bookman', *The Sphere*, 16 May 1925, p. 202; see also E. Wolf and J. F. Fleming, *Rosenbach, a Biography* (London: Weidenfeld and Nicolson, 1960), p. 220.

[238] J. Backhouse, 'The Sale of the Luttrell Psalter', in R. Myers and M. Harris (eds.), *Antiquaries, Book Collectors and the Circles of Learning* (Winchester: Oak Knoll Press, 1996), pp. 113–14.

you a hint to the same effect I should appreciate it more than I can say'.[239] This was a tacit acknowledgement that the American market was small and close-knit. Millar went on to set out the Museum's case: 'You know the importance of the Louttrell Psalter as a national monument, and I am afraid that if it comes into a public auction it will have all the added publicity resulting from its deposit here: it has been in constant use in the Students' Room'. Morgan Jr agreed to loan the museum money to buy the manuscripts at auction, which was to be repaid within a year. If the money could not be raised, the manuscripts would belong to Morgan. As Millar explained: 'Mr. Morgan's avowed object being to save the MSS. if possible for the British Museum, but otherwise to secure them absolutely and beyond all doubt for the Morgan Library'.[240] The departure of the manuscripts was likely to prompt an outcry, but by giving the museum the chance to obtain them Morgan bought himself good publicity and ensured that if anyone else got the books it would be the Morgan Library. Moreover, since most of the probable bidders had been asked not to compete with the museum, Morgan was likely to obtain the books at an excellent price. This plan was not completely unprecedented, as Kenyon claimed that in 1920 Greene had instructed Quaritch to secure the Life of Saint Cuthbert manuscript for the British Museum if the museum was outbid, although in the end this was not necessary.[241] On 29 July 1929 the Luttrell Psalter was withdrawn from the auction and sold privately to the British Museum for £31,500.[242] The museum then bought the Bedford Hours at auction for £33,000.[243] Also in the auction were

---

[239] British Library Add. MS 74095, letter from E. G. Millar to B. Greene, 8 January 1929. See also E. G. Millar, *The Luttrell Psalter* (London: British Museum, 1932); Backhouse, 'Sale of the Luttrell Psalter', p. 118; M. P. Brown, *The Luttrell Psalter: A Facsimile* (London: British Library, 2006), p. 31.

[240] British Library Add. MS 74095, letter from E. G. Millar to B. Greene, 26 July 1929.

[241] F. G. Kenyon, 'A Tribute from the British Museum', in D. Miner (ed.), *Studies in Art and Literature for Belle da Costa Greene* (Princeton: Princeton University Press, 1954), p. 4.

[242] Millar, *Luttrell Psalter*, p. 7; Backhouse, 'Sale of the Luttrell Psalter', p. 124.

[243] Millar, *Luttrell Psalter*, p. 7; Backhouse, 'Sale of the Luttrell Psalter', pp. 124–6.

nine manuscripts belonging to Sir George Holford. Of these, one was bought by Rosenbach, two by Maggs (who immediately resold one to Edith Beatty), and six by Quaritch. One of Quaritch's purchases was for the American Cortland Bishop. Even at this sale, therefore only two of eleven items went immediately to America.

Morgan's gamble on the Luttrell Psalter and Bedford Hours very nearly paid off. On 29 October 1929 the Wall Street Crash triggered a global economic crisis. In this environment it was extremely difficult to raise money, although the museum ran a much larger campaign than it had for the purchase of the St Cuthbert manuscript nine years earlier. Notices appeared in the press and a donation box was installed in the museum next to where the books were on display. By May 1930 the money for the Luttrell Psalter had been raised, but with eleven days until the agreed deadline only £12,300 of the £33,000 needed for the Bedford Psalter-Hours had been found.[244] In the final days, the NACF, which had initially given £7,500, provided a further £8,600 and Morgan agreed to be flexible about the deadline.[245] By October 1930 the money had been paid, and Morgan declared 'the transaction is completed, and I am reconciled'.[246]

2.4 Conclusions

Throughout the period 1890–1929 Americans were identified as major consumers of rare books on the British market. The departure of books for America attracted far more comment than sales to European buyers. Particularly at the start of the period, this cannot have been linked to volume, as large numbers of books left Britain for other destinations. Yet America had a special status because none of the manuscripts and early printed books imported to the country had been made there. At the same time, as 'The Magnet' (Figure 1) illustrated, the book trade could be viewed

---

[244] R. Witt, 'The Bedford Hours', *The Times*, 18 July 1930, p. 10; Backhouse, 'Sale of the Luttrell Psalter', p. 125.

[245] E. G. Millar, 'The Luttrell Psalter and the Bedford Book of Hours', *The British Museum Quarterly*, 5(2) (1930), pp. 45–6.

[246] British Library Add. MS 74095, letter from J. P. Morgan Jr. to E. G. Millar, 27 October 1930.

as part of a much wider transportation of works of art and items of cultural heritage across the Atlantic. This resulted in America and Americans (in the abstract) being presented as a threat to British collectors and institutions.

In reality, a small number of American buyers were increasing prices for rare books through their commissions at auctions, as well as buying from British dealers' stock. Not all these Americans were based in America. Notably Wellcome and Beatty housed their collections in London (as did Morgan until the completion of his New York library building). However, Morgan, Huntington, and Walters built large collections destined to become public museums in America, giving another dimension to their reputations and equipping the younger nation. The result of higher prices for certain types of material, including illuminated manuscripts and early printed books, was a windfall for British sellers. Since these men were of the class that also wrote for, edited, and owned newspapers, it is unsurprising that public protest was muted, with Shorter in particular providing a prolonged defence of the trade with America. However, the growth of a small number of prominent American collections threw into relief the struggles faced by British institutions in competing for particular items.

In response to the challenges faced in the auction room, some collectors and institutions sought other ways to obtain material. Although Huth's bequest was exceptional, museum staff, including Cockerell, Gilson, and Millar, used their networks to encourage gifts or opportunities to buy off the open market. The Beattys also used their contacts to secure private sales. In addition, the NACF contributed to the purchase of some exceptional illuminated books, although requests for support far outstripped its means. Ultimately, the appeal of the dollar was irresistible, particularly after the enormous expense of the First World War. The British government took no steps to restrict exports and provided a limited budget for purchases for the 'national' collections. Against this backdrop, Partridge's cartoon resonated because a contemporary reader would have understood that Shakespeare's ghost was justified in his fears.

3 The Book-Brokers

The movement of rare books and manuscripts across the Atlantic was facilitated by dealers (including auctioneers and those with bookshops) who were sometimes described in America as book-brokers. In addition to selling books and buying on commission at auction, dealers exchanged books amongst themselves, created and distributed catalogues, offered advice, provided valuations for probate, and arranged transportation. Dealers had to maintain discretion and client confidence while at the same time making a name for their business. In late-nineteenth-century London, Bernard Quaritch provided a model that later booksellers sought to emulate; at his death in 1899, obituaries described him as the king of booksellers and likened him to Napoleon.[247] Yet in addition to prompting parallels with heroic figures, booksellers on both sides of the Atlantic were recognisable figures in their own right. During a Hoe sale in 1912 *The New York Herald* published a cartoon by J. Norman Lynd entitled 'The Bloodless Battles for Books of the Bibliophiles', caricaturing eight of the buyers, including Abraham Rosenbach, George D. Smith, and Bernard Alfred Quaritch, together with the auctioneers Major Emory Turner and Arthur Swann (Figure 3). These studies exaggerated the distinctive appearance of some of those bidding at the Hoe sale, while in the centre of the page 'the shades of Grolier, Gutenberg and Aldus' stood wide-eyed and open-mouthed at the prices for their creations. Yet by showing the dealers squeezed into chairs too small for them, the cartoonist suggested both the larger-than-life reputations of these individuals and a unity of occupation, which found a parallel in the co-operation within the trade that saw dealers exchanging books, acting as agents for one another, and, in London at least, collaborating to suppress prices at auction.

Although now mostly less well known than collectors who founded libraries, book-brokers shaped the transatlantic trade on multiple levels. They cultivated the growing American clientele, providing catalogues,

---

[247] See for example: 'The King of Booksellers', *The Daily Telegraph & Courier*, 20 December 1899, p. 3; Napoleon: 'Obituary', *The Times*, 19 December 1899, p. 6.

Figure 3 J. N. Lynd, 'The Bloodless Battles for Books of the Bibliophiles', *The New York Herald*, 14 January 1912

advice, and information about books and the market. In addition, book-sellers crafted narratives around books, to help them appeal to specific clients. Within some of these stories, dealers cast themselves in heroic roles, finding books in far-away places or hostile environments. Yet book-brokers also dealt with the mundane aspects of the business, including packing and shipping. Their role was crucial in ensuring books got safely to their new homes but also shaped attitudes to books and the transatlantic trade.

3.1 Cultivating a Market

In 1890 Alfred Quaritch's American tour was designed to encourage a developing market. The introduction to the catalogue for his exhibition announced 'that the books and manuscripts now collected for exhibition will, in America, attract the attention of a number of appreciative visitors far greater than it would be possible to draw to such a display in Europe', suggesting that it was part of the dealer's business to attract customers.[248] The trip was expensive and risky. Despite the flattery offered by the catalogue, sales were small and came mostly from existing clients.[249] Yet Alfred was able to meet his customers in their own environment, visiting Theodore Irwin's home in Oswego, and to encounter new potential buyers, many of whom subsequently spent large sums with the firm. While Alfred's letters expressed frustration, grumbling that 'my ambition is to make plenty of money, but this trade certainly doesn't seem to promise it', his father took a long view, declaring 'Do not be low-spirited; if we do not sell the books now, we sell them later on'.[250]

In the 1890s the American market for rare books was not solely dependent on European booksellers. Some Americans had already estab-lished themselves in London as exporters of books. These included Benjamin Franklin Stevens, who had been in London since 1860 (where he was a despatch agent for the US government), and Alexander Denham, who moved to London in the late 1880s. Denham died in 1902 and his sons

---

[248] Quaritch, *Exhibition of Books*, p. vi. [249] See Introduction.

[250] London, Bernard Quaritch Ltd., letter from B. A. Quaritch to his father dated 21 February 1890; Oxford, Bodleian Library, MS Eng. Lett. c. 435, f. 88.

Frederick and Waring took over the business. However, the subsequent fate of Denham's firm demonstrates how challenging the market was in this period and in particular the problem of cash-flow for the day-to-day running of the business when capital was tied up in stock. On 18 December 1902, Frederick Denham visited Quaritch's shop claiming that he had an American customer who wanted to buy copies of the First and Second Folio editions of Shakespeare. What followed was documented in court records.[251] Denham asked to take Quaritch's copy of the Second Folio to show his client and Quaritch agreed, adding that he wanted a decision on the sale within twenty-four hours. The price was £720, which was at the upper end of what someone, for example, an American visitor to London in a hurry might be expected to pay. When Denham did not return, Quaritch assumed the book had been sold and that Denham would pay him within a month. This was not an unusual arrangement, as booksellers often extended credit to one another.

Instead, Denham took the book to another bookseller, Frank Sabin (whose father Joseph moved to New York from Oxford when Frank was a baby, creating another family business that spanned the Atlantic). According to Sabin, Denham asked him if he wanted to buy a Second Folio Shakespeare, as Denham was short of funds for another purchase. Sabin was not enthusiastic, but gave Denham a cheque for £400 for the Second Folio and two other books, with the option of buying the books back for £440. This too was not an uncommon arrangement, in which booksellers helped each other with cash flow in exchange for a modest profit, but Sabin did not know that the book belonged to Quaritch. In a further twist, J. & J. Leighton's ledgers record that on that day they sold Denham two medieval manuscripts, perhaps bought with Sabin's money or convinced by his cheque that Denham's credit was good.[252] Denham

---

[251] *Old Bailey Proceedings Online* (www.oldbaileyonline.org, version 8.0, 11 September 2021), April 1904, trial of Frederick Denham (34) (t19040418-384). See also A. L. Schwarz, *Dear Mr. Cockerell, Dear Mr. Peirce: An Annotated Description of the Correspondence of Sydney C. Cockerell and Harold Peirce in the Grolier Club Archive* (High Wycombe: Rivendale Press, 2006).

[252] British Library, Add. MS 45163.

returned to Sabin's shop on 31 December to repurchase the Shakespeare, leaving a cheque which was later refused by the bank. Denham then proceeded with the Shakespeare to Leighton, where he tried the same trick, now asking £400 for the book. Leighton agreed to pay £350, giving Denham the right to buy the book back for £400 within ten days. A book that could plausibly be sold to a collector for £720 was worth less than half that price to a fellow dealer.

Alexander Denham's illness and death earlier in the year probably contributed to a crisis in the business, leading his son to take increasingly desperate measures. From the subsequent court records and newspaper reports it appears that the Shakespeare was not the only book that Denham had, in effect, pawned to other dealers, making a loss each time he redeemed a book, but maintaining an illusion of having ready cash.[253] The following year he was tried for obtaining goods and credit after his bankruptcy, obtaining credit by fraud, disposing of property otherwise than in the ordinary way of his trade and fraudulently converting to his own use property entrusted to him. Quaritch, Sabin, and Leighton all testified to their connection with the Shakespeare, and representatives of Denham's bank bore witness to problems with insufficient credit to meet his cheques. Denham was found guilty and sentenced to nine months imprisonment, after which he seems to have returned to New York.

Although men like Quaritch and Smith became rich from their businesses, the Denham case is a reminder that the trade was precarious, with most books only returning small profits. Quaritch's standard commission for purchasing an item at auction was 10 per cent, but institutions and some clients were charged just 5 per cent. Seymour de Ricci asserted that Bernard Quaritch died with 'hardly a penny to his name', owning 'the finest stock in the world' of the books he loved, but Quaritch's estate was valued at £38,782 gross and £19,712 net (making him a multi-millionaire by today's standards).[254] While it was often claimed that booksellers would not sell

---

[253] 'Option Book Sales', *The Daily Telegraph & Courier*, 19 January 1904, p. 6; 'Fraudulent Dealings in Rare Books', *The Globe*, 23 April 1904, p. 3.

[254] S. de Ricci, *English Collectors of Books & Manuscripts (1530–1930) and their Marks of Ownership* (reprinted: Bloomington: Indiana University Press, 1960), p. 165.

books to clients they believed unworthy of them, in reality, as Bernard Quaritch pointed out in 1884, it was good business 'to be friendly with everybody'.[255] Even more bluntly, Smith was frequently described as not being interested in books except as commodities.[256] Whether or not dealers cared for books as objects, they needed to know how to make money from them, which relied, in part, on being able to assess what they were, who might buy them and for how much.

In addition to selling stock and taking commissions, dealers nurtured relationships with clients, offering advice, sending notice of books that might interest them, drawing their attention to forthcoming sales, providing estimates of what items might raise at auction, and sharing gossip. For example, in 1926 Rosenbach courted staff of the New York Public Library, aware that the Spencer Committee had money to spend. In February he offered the Liesborn Gospels, an early medieval illuminated manuscript in a treasure binding, for 'a special price to the Library of $47,500.00 net'.[257] The library did not buy, but undaunted Rosenbach tried again in April, offering a fifteenth-century manuscript he described as 'Arthur of Little Britain', once again for a 'special price', this time $64,850.[258] Rosenbach stressed the rarity, literary, and historical value of the manuscript, adding 'Neither the British Museum nor the Bodleian, both great manuscript depositories, possesses any codex of this romance'.[259] In order to make the cost palatable, Rosenbach argued that 'One really great acquisition such as this, though it exclude others for a time, would confer an extra-distinction on the Spencer Library that many minor pieces could not give it'. Evidently

[255] 'A Chat about Books with Mr. Quaritch', *Pall Mall Gazette*, 19 December 1884, p. 6. For an example of a claim that Quaritch sought worthy clients: 'Literary Gossip', *Globe*, 23 December 1899, p. 6.

[256] See, for example, J. Drinkwater, *A Book for Bookmen* (New York: George H. Doran, 1927), p. 207.

[257] Philadelphia, Rosenbach Museum Archive, letter from A. S. W. Rosenbach to Dr Lydenberg, 2 February 1926.

[258] Ibid., letter from A. S. W. Rosenbach to E. H. Anderson, 1 April 1926.

[259] Ibid., letter from A. S. W. Rosenbach to the Spencer Fund Committee, 9 April 1926.

convinced, the library acquired the book.[260] Although the final decision rested with the purchasers, therefore, dealers helped to shape collections by offering some books and not others. In this, institutional memory could be extremely valuable. For example, in 1932 when Belle Greene hesitated over sending commissions for the sale of Beatty's manuscripts, Quaritch's manager, Frederick Fergusson wrote to remind her that when the Mostyn Gospels had been sold to Beatty in 1920 she had sent a commission for it and 'cabled afterwards asking if this MS. could still be had'.[261] Greene was convinced and the manuscript went to New York.

Indeed the distinction between dealer and expert advisor was not always clear-cut. Cockerell, who had been introduced to rare books through his work for William Morris, considered becoming a dealer and sought advice from Quaritch and others.[262] Instead he opted to work part-time for Yates Thompson, cataloguing manuscripts, bidding for items at auction, and arranging for private purchases. In 1900–1 Cockerell also brokered the sale of manuscripts to the Boston Public Library, although by 1904 when he was helping arrange sales for Charles Fairfax Murray he invoked the rhetoric of not wanting to see books go to America, an argument he made again when Yates Thompson announced the sale of his manuscripts in 1918.[263] By then, Cockerell was firmly embedded in the British cultural establishment, as director of the Fitzwilliam Museum.

In 1919 when Greene was looking for someone to write a catalogue of manuscripts, Dring recommended the retired Keeper of Manuscripts at the

---

[260] The manuscript is now New York Public Library, MS Spencer 34.

[261] New York, Morgan Library Archive, MCC 1310 Quaritch XI, letter from F. S. Fergusson to B. Greene, 13 May 1932. The Mostyn Gospels is now New York, Morgan Library, M.777.

[262] C. de Hamel, 'Cockerell as Entrepreneur', *The Book Collector*, 55(1) (2006), pp. 49–72.

[263] W. P. Stoneman, '"Variously Employed": The Pre-Fitzwilliam Career of Sydney Carlyle Cockerell', *Transactions of the Cambridge Bibliographical Society*, 13(4) (2007), 345–62; Herrmann, *Sotheby's*, p. 187; British Library, Add. MS 52755, ff. 210–12, draft letter to Yates Thompson dated 24 January 1918; see also J. Q. Bennett, 'Portman Square to New Bond Street, or How to Make Money Though Rich', *The Book Collector*, 16(3) (1967), pp. 323–39; Schwarz, *Dear Mr. Cockerell*; Section 2.1.

British Museum, Sir George Warner.[264] It was not unknown for those employed in museums and universities to work for private collectors. M. R. James produced volumes for members of the Roxburghe Club as well as a catalogue of Morgan's manuscripts and early printed books, published in 1906, and catalogues for Cambridge colleges. In 1923 Millar, then working for the British Museum, was hired by Beatty to 'assist me in a general way in my library at odd times and drop in at Sotheby's when convenient to you and generally follow the question of manuscripts for me' and the following year Millar began work on a catalogue of Beatty's manuscripts.[265] Millar's contacts among private collectors, including Greene and Beatty, proved extremely helpful in 1929 when the British Museum sought to buy the Luttrell Psalter.[266] Similarly, the connections made by Alfred Quaritch and others in the 1890s laid the foundations for an important transatlantic network of collectors, scholars, and dealers that formed a significant part of the trade in rare books in the early decades of the following century.

3.2 Selling Stories

Dealers thought carefully about what American clients might want to buy. In the catalogue for the 1890 American exhibition, Bernard Quaritch declared it unnecessary to explain the sections on English literature, 'as it is better known in America than in England', and Americana.[267] The following year, Alfred's stock on his American visit included a letter written by Christopher Columbus, containing an account of the discovery of America, although Quaritch failed to sell it on that trip. At the same time, booksellers crafted stories around individual works. One reporter described Quaritch's 1890 exhibition as being 'like a peep at Fairyland'.[268] He claimed that Quaritch had recounted to him a history of the Golden Gospels, which included

---

[264] New York, Morgan Library Archive, MCC 1310 Quaritch VII, letter from E. H. Dring to B. Greene, 17 July 1919.

[265] Dublin, Chester Beatty Library Archives, Millar Correspondence, letter from A. C. Beatty to E. G. Millar, 6 November 1923.

[266] See Section 2.3.   [267] Quaritch, *Exhibition of Books*, p. xv.

[268] J. P. Bocock, 'Book World Wonders', *The Pittsburgh Dispatch*, 26 January 1890, p. 4.

it having been written for the Emperor Charlemagne, before being presented to King Henry VIII of England by the pope, and later passing through the collections of 'a Scotch nobleman', the Duke of Hamilton, the Imperial Library of Berlin and 'M. Didot, the great Parisian biblio-phile'. An American owner would therefore be joining a remarkable litany of former owners from European cultural centres. In a similar vein, following his success with the 'Little Arthur' manuscript, in October 1926 Rosenbach tried to interest The New York Public Library in a fourteenth-century Sachsenspiegel manuscript. He wrote:

> Not only is it a manuscript of rare beauty but it is intrinsi-cally one of the most valuable in existence. European scho-lars regard it as the finest of all Hapsburg manuscripts, and it is the only Hapsburg manuscript in this country. It is a matter of record that the city of Vienna was eager to purchase it but that it lacked the funds.[269]

The manuscript had been bought by Smith at the Huth sale in 1918 for £140 ($700). In 1926, Rosenbach offered the New York Public Library a discounted price of $6,750. On this occasion the committee of the New York Public Library was unconvinced and the book appears to have remained in Rosenbach's stock until sold to the Library of Congress in 1946.[270]

The idea of an elite, though usually vague, provenance was often used by the dealer Wilfrid Voynich. In 1904 Voynich was profiled in *The Tatler*, which declared that his stock was worth £25,000.[271] At that time Voynich was developing a reputation for finding rare books on the continent, telling *The Tatler* that he bought 'what he requires from Government collec-tions or monastic institutions in out-of-the-way places'. However, he also bought books from London dealers. In 1914, plausibly fearing the consequences for his life in London and disrupted access to the

---

[269] Philadelphia, Rosenbach Museum Archive, RCo. I:129:32, letter from A. S. W. Rosenbach to H. M. Lydenberg, 5 October 1926.

[270] Washington, DC, Library of Congress, MS 12.

[271] 'Concerning a Great Bookseller whose Wife Writes Good Books', *The Tatler*, 25 May 1904, p. 309.

continent caused by the First World War, but also attracted by the potential of the American market, Voynich turned his eyes to the United States. In November that year he set off for New York with a collection of rare books and manuscripts including the cipher manuscript for which he is now best known.[272] In America, he teased the press with the romance of his manuscripts' origins, declaring that,

> Through papers which came into his possession, he learned
> of the existence of a large number of valuable manuscripts
> in Austria, which had been hastily removed from central
> Italy at the time of Napoleon's first invasion in the last
> decade of the eighteenth century. They were at last found
> in a castle belonging to a distinguished member of the
> nobility. Their existence was unknown to the owner. The
> chests in which they were stored had not been opened for
> over a century.[273]

Yet not all his manuscripts had come from continental Europe, as a set of full-page images, probably made to preface a Psalter, sold to the Art Institute of Chicago, had appeared in the famous exhibition at the Burlington Fine Arts Club in London in 1908, when it was part of the Huth collection.[274] Moreover, the Austrian castle was later revealed to be cover for purchases made from the Jesuits.[275]

Voynich was also fond of optimistic attributions to well-known authors or artists. Another of the manuscripts taken on his American tour in 1914–1915 was a volume of lives of the desert fathers with miniatures said to be

[272]　Now New Haven, Beinecke Library, MS 408.

[273]　'Manuscripts of Rare Value at Albright Art Gallery', *Buffalo Courier*, 6 December 1915, p. 5.

[274]　Now Chicago, Art Institute, 1915.533; S. C. Cockerell, *Burlington Fine Arts Club; Exhibition of Illuminated Manuscripts* (London: Chiswick Press, 1908), p. 27, no. 57.

[275]　We are grateful to René Zandbergen for discussion of this topic; see also New Haven, Beinecke Library, Correspondence concerning MS 408 cipher manuscript, letter by E. Voynich, 19 July 1930.

attributed to Giotto or Lorenzetto. In 1916 he sold the manuscript to the Morgan Library, reportedly for $70,000.[276] It is no longer attributed to either artist. Similarly, the American enthusiasm for Shakespeare helped to contribute to high prices for works that were unlikely to be from his pen. In 1919 Smith paid £200 for a 1619 copy of *Sir John Oldcastle* attributed to Shakespeare and £130 for *A Yorkshire Tragedie*, described in Sotheby's catalogue as a 'doubtful Shakespearean Play'.[277] Well-known names, whether owners, authors, or artists could prove attractive to collectors.

It is important not to overlook the symbiosis between dealers and scholars, and there could be a close relationship between commercially-motivated rhetoric and scholarly publications. Dealers' catalogues were one means of disseminating descriptions of books, and ideas expressed there could have a significant impact.[278] When Huntington purchased the Towneley Plays manuscript in 1922 for £3,400, it became one of the most expensive English medieval drama manuscripts ever sold. Yet the manuscript had a relatively short critical history dominated by early commercial assessments. Martin Stevens noted that 'Like so many other prized books of the Middle Ages, the unique manuscript of the *Towneley Plays* has suffered, until very recently, from the benign neglect of its scholars'.[279] The first printed reference to the manuscript appeared in 1814 in a R. H. Evans sale catalogue. The information contained in that catalogue initiated a conversation between dealers and scholars that lasted for over a century. Since from a commercial point of view, a 'touch of monkish

---

[276] 'Ancient Papers to be Shown', *The Detroit Times*, 11 April 1915, p. 9; 'City News in Brief', *The Detroit Times*, 11 April 1917, p. 3; see also A. Hunt, 'Foreign Dealers in the English Trade', in Mandelbrote (ed.), *Out of Print & Into Profit*, pp. 245–69, 253; the manuscript is now New York, Morgan Library, M.626.

[277] *Catalogue of a Most Important & Interesting Collection of Early English Plays the Property of the Lord Mostyn [. . .] Sold by Auction [. . .] On Thursday, the 20th of March, 1919, and Following Day* (London: Sotheby, Wilkinson & Hodge, 1919), lots 299–300.

[278] J. Carter, 'Bibliography and the Rare Book Trade', *The Papers of the Bibliographical Society of America*, 48(3) (1954), p. 225.

[279] M. Stevens, 'The History of the *Towneley Plays*: Its History and Editions', *The Papers of the Bibliographical Society of America*, 67(3) (1973), p. 231.

romance did not come amiss', the cataloguer connected the manuscript to the Abbey of Widkirk.[280] Questions regarding this connection arose, but – and this demonstrates the potential for catalogue entries to shape textual understandings – the plays nonetheless came to be commonly referred to as the 'Widkirk Plays'.

The Towneley manuscript appeared for sale again with Evans in 1815 and 1819, the same description used each time, allowing the information to 'acquire benchmark status'.[281] These entries carried sufficient authority for the Surtees Society to respond directly to their claims in their 1836 edition of the plays, stating that: there 'is nothing known with certainty respecting any previous ownership', and that there 'is no place called Widkirk in the neighbourhood of Wakefield, and neither there nor in any part of England was there ever an Abbey of Widkirk'.[282] This conversation continued in a series of Quaritch catalogues. Quaritch purchased the manuscript for stock in 1883, and the manuscript appeared in six catalogues between 1884 and 1900. While the price and dating of the manuscript changed slightly across the six entries, a focus on the ongoing negotiation between scholars and cataloguers remained consistent. Quaritch's readers learned that there remained some debate over where the manuscript was produced, where the plays were performed, and how the manuscript was acquired by the Towneley family. The Quaritch entries even directly questioned claims made by the Surtees Society edition and bluntly acknowledged that 'whether Woodkirk or Wakefield be the spot in which this volume was produced – and the two places are not far apart – the MS. remains a wonderful and

---

[280] M. Twycross, 'They Did Not Come Out of an Abbey in Lancashire: Francis Douce and the Manuscript of the Towneley Plays', *Medieval English Theatre*, 37 (2015), p. 156; R. H. Evans, 'Bibliotheca Towneleiana: A Catalogue of the Curious and Extensive Library of the Late John Towneley, Esq.', 8 June 1814, Part I, p. 45, no. 894.

[281] Twycross, 'They Did Not Come Out of an Abbey', p. 157.

[282] J. Hunter, 'Preface', in *The Towneley Mysteries*, Surtees Society (London: J. B. Nichols, 1836), pp. v–xviii, ix.

priceless monument of old English dramatic literature'.[283] It was priced at £820.

Despite all the uncertainty surrounding the Towneley manuscript's provenance, Quaritch eventually sold it to Sir Edward Coates in 1900 (the sale price listed in the 1899 catalogue was £700). When the manuscript re-entered the market in 1922, Sotheby's published the longest and most detailed sales entry to appear in connection with the manuscript, complete with added information from the Early English Text Society's 1897 reprinting of the plays. Interestingly, the entry also stated that the manuscript was 'traditionally associated with Widkirk or Woodkirk', demonstrating how commercial claims can actively participate in the production of artefactual meaning.[284] Today the manuscript is linked to neither Widkirk nor Woodkirk. However, even E. P. Goldschmidt was not overly concerned about the accuracy of cataloguers' claims, arguing that it 'is the privilege of the bookseller to advance a bold hypothesis that will enhance the interest of his books as long as it is plausible. Not on him, but on the coolly sceptical historian rests the duty to demolish what can not be strictly demonstrated'.[285] As much as commercial rhetoric could resemble bibliographical research, it should not be mistaken for such.

The stories Voynich told about his books were part of a larger narrative about himself. It is probably not coincidental that Voynich's partner (and from 1902 his wife) Ethel Boole was a well-known novelist.[286] The couple's stories about Voynich's early life included his escape from exile in Siberia and having started his business with a borrowed shilling, although the success of Ethel's novel *The Gadfly* around the time Voynich was establishing himself suggests an

[283] B. Quaritch, *Catalogue of English Literature, Poetic, Dramatic, Historic, Miscellaneous* (London: Bernard Quaritch, 1884), p. 2132, no. 21885.

[284] *Catalogue of the Towneley Mysteries and the York Missal, the Property of the Late Sir Edward F. Coates, BT., M.P. [. . .] Sold by Auction [. . .] On Wednesday, the 8th of February, 1922* (London: Sotheby, Wilkinson & Hodge, 1922), p. 5.

[285] E. P. Goldschmidt, 'The Study of Early Bookbinding', in *The Bibliographical Society, 1892–1942*, p. 178.

[286] 'Concerning a Great Bookseller', p. 309.

alternative source of income.[287] In 1902 Ethel told the press that the couple had been 'so much annoyed by Russian spies that we were obliged to ask the English government for protection', and that story appeared in papers in America.[288] Voynich also reinvented himself to suit his business. On the passenger list for his voyage to America in 1916 he was described as an art expert.[289] Similarly, in that year the *American Art News* reported that Voynich was to 'deliver a course of lectures on his speciality of old illuminated and art illustrated Mss. and books in universities of the middle west', and that 'He has brought with him [...] a further large selection from his collection of illuminated Mss. and precious books'.[290]

Voynich may have been inspired to try his luck in America, in part, by Smith's much-publicised visit to London in the summer of 1914. By that time, Smith was adept at using the press to promote himself. In May 1914 an account of his rags-to-riches story circulated in the American papers.[291] From London, Smith sent bulletins to *The New York Times* detailing his record expenditure. Much of his language suggested that he was engaged in a fight. In July he reported, 'Have had a very successful trip. It was a long and hard battle, but I won out O. K.'.[292] In particular, Smith cast himself as the victor in a war against the London dealers. American papers reported that he had smashed the British dealers' 'ring'. This was a practice whereby dealers did not compete for items that they did not hold commissions for,

---

[287] G. Kennedy, *The Booles & Hintons: Two Dynasties that Helped Shape the Modern World* (Cork: Atrium, 2016), p. 222.

[288] For example, 'The Nobleman and the Spy', *Arizona Republic*, 21 December 1902, p. 11.

[289] Kew, The National Archives, BT27 Board of Trade: Commercial and Statistical Department and Successors: Outwards Passenger Lists, 13 May 1916, SS. St Louis.

[290] 'General Art News', *American Art News*, 14(9), 12 February 1916, p. 3.

[291] For example, 'Fortunes in Old Books', *The Kansas City Times*, 20 May 1914, p. 5, but this was probably not the original source and the story was widely reproduced in other papers.

[292] 'Smith Pleased with Books', *NYT*, 25 July 1914, p. 2.

allowing them to be bought for low prices.[293] Further auctions would then be held in a local pub by the members of the ring to establish what they thought the item's real value was. The difference in price – which was assumed to be the successful bidder's profit – was then split between the group's members. Smith refused to join the ring and declared that by paying high prices he had defeated it. The truth is almost certainly more complicated. By buying large quantities of stock at high prices Smith was preventing the ring from obtaining items on which they could make shared profits. In addition, he contributed to the general bidding, forcing dealers to pay higher prices than they might have intended, although since we do not have a record of every bid this is tricky to quantify. However, by helping to set new record prices, he potentially increased the price that could be asked for books already in London booksellers' stock and bookselling is a long game. The ring may have been frustrated by Smith's participation at the biggest sales of the season, but he was only in London for a short time and, perhaps most importantly, not all his purchases were out of line with the prices of a few months earlier. He did, after all, have his own profits to consider.

3.3 Practicalities

There was more to dealing in books than simply making record bids at auction or traveling to Europe in search of undiscovered rarities. Catalogues had to be produced, potentially requiring research, and correspondence dealt with. Books might need repair or rebinding to make them attractive to new owners. The larger firms employed staff to help with specialist tasks from cataloguing to packing and transportation. Moreover, dealers fulfilled other roles, including offering valuations for collections, which gave them advance notice of what was coming onto the market. These activities provided opportunities, but sometimes required great diplomacy. For example, in 1927 Dring valued Sir George Holford's library for probate and advised Greene that the collection was likely to be sold,

---

[293] See F. Herrmann, 'The Role of the Auction Houses', in Mandelbrote (ed.), *Out of Print & Into Profit*, p. 13.

hinting that the British Museum would probably want a twelfth-century illuminated Life of St Edmund.[294] Although Greene agreed that the Life of St Edmund ought to go to the museum, she also asked: 'is there a possibility (without breaking a confidence) for you to give Mr Morgan and myself a general idea of the appraised value'?[295] It is extremely unlikely that Dring would have been able to supply such information without breaking confidence, but he deflected the question observing 'it would not be any guidance if I gave you an idea of the valuation I made of them. It was purely a valuation for probate and both you and especially Mr. Morgan know quite well that when valuing for probate I place as small a value as I can on the various items'.[296] This practice would have helped to reduce the tax burden on the estate thus Dring's work allowed him to serve multiple clients at the same time. Despite Greene's claims that the St Edmund manuscript ought to go to the British Museum, when it became clear that Holford's executors were not prepared to offer it to the museum on preferential terms, she secured the book for the Morgan Library.

Similarly, Greene could play dealers off against each other. In 1930, Greene reported to Fergusson that 'Most confidentially, Dr. Rosenbach thought this one [a book by Miguel de Cervantes] in such bad condition that we ought not to retain it' and was promptly offered a discounted price.[297] Although Fergusson protested that 'It is all very well for Dr. Rosenbach to think that it is in too bad a condition for you to keep, but he knows very well the rarity of the book and, [. . .] the last copy which he bought from me a few years ago had considerably more of the title in facsimile than this has', both the sale and his relationship with Greene were worth preserving, particularly as Greene declared that she was returning all the other books he had sent.[298]

[294] New York, Morgan Library Archive, MCC 1310 Quaritch X, letter from E. H. Dring to B. Greene, 3 May 1927. The manuscript is now New York, Morgan Library, M.736.

[295] Ibid., letter from B. Greene to E. H. Dring, 12 May 1927.

[296] Ibid., letter from E. H. Dring to B. Greene, 27 May 1927.

[297] New York, Morgan Library Archive, ARC 1310 MCC Quaritch XI, letter from B. Greene to F. S. Fergusson, October 1930.

[298] Ibid., letter from F. S. Fergusson to B. Greene, 17 October 1930.

The transatlantic trade had the particular challenge of international shipping. Voynich's records detail the costs of transporting books from London to New York, which in 1926 included expenses for packing books into trunks, taxis to the station, the fare to Victoria Docks, excess luggage charges, and tips to porters, the elevator girl, taxis, and the man who weighed the luggage.[299] In 1927 Dring reported to Greene that 'the limit of weight to the parcel post to America is now raised to twenty-two pounds, which will mean an enormous saving in freight to America and will militate very strongly against the 1½% ad valorem rates which the Cunard and other English steamers charge on high-priced consignments'.[300] Smith found ways to make even such mundane activities newsworthy. In 1914, following the declaration of war, the *Chicago Tribune* reported that Smith entrusted $35,000 of books to the former champion boxer Abe Attel, who travelled with them in a stateroom, while American millionaires desperate to escape Europe took places in steerage.[301] Yet despite attempts by dealers on both sides of the Atlantic to project glamour onto the trade through newspaper reports, bookselling involved much unseen labour, often for little or no immediate reward.

3.4 A Two-Way Trade

Voynich's business records shed further light on the claims made by Shorter and Rosenbach that the British could buy back books from the United States and the idea that America was a voracious market.[302] Every book that Voynich imported to America for stock was given a new number in an ascending sequence. The reappearance of low numbers on inventories from the 1920s indicates that they moved back and forth between London and New York. For example, a thirteenth-century Psalter given the number A1655 was shipped to New York by Voynich in 1920, 1923, and 1924.

---

[299] New York, Grolier Club, Voynich Papers, 'Expenses in Re Return to New York, via SS. Minnetonka, November 6. 1926'.

[300] New York, Morgan Library Archive, MCC 1310 Quaritch X, letter from E. H. Dring to B. Greene, 26 July 1927.

[301] 'Abe Attel "Books" Passage', *The Chicago Daily Tribune*, 6 August 1914, p. 14.

[302] See Introduction.

Remaining unsold at Voynich's death in 1930, it was sent back to London to be sold at auction.[303] Similarly a fifteenth-century manuscript of *De Re Militari*, with the stock number A38, which was presumably part of the stock brought to America in 1914, was reimported in 1924 and 1925.[304] This demonstrates both that Voynich's stock travelled widely and that even in the 1920s not every book was immediately snapped up by an American collector.

The fate of some of the books from Hoe's library confirms that the international trade was not solely in one direction. At the first part of the Hoe sale in 1911, Quaritch's clients included Americans, meaning that not all his purchases went to Britain. However, at the later parts of the sale in 1912 Quaritch and his assistants bought books and manuscripts for stock, including several manuscripts subsequently sold to Beatty. Most of these manuscripts had been acquired by Hoe in continental Europe, but at least one Book of Hours (now Philadelphia Museum of Art 1945–65–17) had been purchased from Quaritch by Hoe. Some of these books returned to America following the sale of part of Beatty's collection in 1932–1933, including the Book of Hours now in the Philadelphia Museum of Art and the de Levis Hours now in the Beinecke Library.[305]

Yet Rosenbach's claims that books could be repurchased by the British were made in the context of a dominant transfer of books from Britain (and elsewhere) to America. In 1927, he noted the recent demand for English material from universities, a market also cultivated by Voynich, arguing that nothing short of the intervention of the British government could counteract the economics of American demand and British supply.[306] Moreover, the idea that rich collectors would be able to buy books in American shops sat awkwardly with Rosenbach's celebration of collectors

---

[303] The manuscript is now New York, Morgan Library, G.2.

[304] The manuscript is now Washington, DC, Library of Congress, Rosenwald ms. no. 13.

[305] Philadelphia Museum of Art 1945–65–17; New Haven, Beinecke Library, MS 400.

[306] Rosenbach, 'Why America Buys', p. 459.

including Huntington, Folger, and the Elizabethan Club at Yale University, whose possessions have not returned to the market.[307]

3.5 Conclusions

The movement of rare books and manuscripts between Britain and America, with some books crossing the ocean multiple times, was underpinned by the book-brokers who transferred books amongst themselves as well as selling them to clients. In the 1890s American and British dealers on both sides of the Atlantic nurtured the market for rare books in America. This involved the movement of people as well as books, with Alfred Quaritch's visits to America and the presence of American dealers in London. While some dealers were motivated by their love of books, successful dealers also needed to be financially astute and to build relationships with their clients. In part, this was done through a shared knowledge of rare books, and dealers' shops, letters, and catalogues all became means of communicating ideas about books and the trade. Most of this work was not glamorous, requiring detailed record-keeping, as well as the practicalities of packing and transporting books. Yet in the American press in particular, booksellers attempted to publicise the drama and spectacle of the trade, from Quaritch's 'fairyland'-like exhibition, to Smith and Rosenbach's record-breaking triumphs in the auction rooms. Moreover, like some of the famous collectors, some dealers created institutions that preserve their names: Quaritch's business is still trading, Voynich's cipher manuscript is typically known simply as the 'Voynich manuscript', and the Rosenbach Museum in Philadelphia preserves both Rosenbach's books and his firm's archives.

[307] Ibid., 456.

Conclusion: Constructing Cultural Histories

From the material presented here, the answer to the question raised in *The Tatler* in 1924 of whether the value of books and *objets d'art* shifts in different context is a resounding yes. Not only did rare books and manuscripts represent different things in Britain and America, but they were understood differently by buyers, sellers, dealers, scholars, and journalists. The enthusiastic public rhetoric surrounding the most famous private American libraries depicted them as sites of national identity. These libraries were often regarded as spaces where modernity could be read through the lens of the past, as emergent American wealth was used to acquire rare books representative of English history, art, and culture. The perceived cultural value of many of these books was echoed by some Britons, who publicly lamented their departure, but British sellers also met American demand by putting a financial value on books. Moreover, some commentators suggested that Britain's role as a source of desirable historic objects, including books, was a source of cultural power. The choices made by all those involved in the rare book trade shaped where and how we now encounter many pre-modern books.

It is no accident that many American institutions were built during a period of explosive capitalist development. T. J. Jackson Lears has argued that antimodernist sentiment was one product of the cultural and social transformations of the late nineteenth and early twentieth centuries. Such anti-modern feelings impacted the middle and upper classes, as medieval 'peasants, saints, and seers haunted American imaginations', providing a form of escapism from the growing pressures of modernity.[308] Specific features of the Middle Ages, such as heraldry and Gothic architecture, came to function as collective symbols 'for an emerging national bourgeoisie' underpinned by pervasive feelings of Anglophilia.[309] It could be argued that medieval manuscripts filled an equally symbolic role. Within major libraries, as in other American institutional spaces, collections of pre-modern objects became emblematic of upper-class cultural authority: assert-

---

[308] Jackson Lears, *No Place of Grace*, pp. xv, 142.   [309] Ibid., 301.

ing both the wealth of collectors and their role as national tastemakers.[310] More recently, bibliographer and collector G. T. Tanselle has referred to collecting as 'a prime example of behavior in which private desire and social gain are mutually supportive'.[311]

The American press persistently hinted that the buying campaigns of collectors represented nationalistic efforts to reunite Americans with their own – frequently threatened – textual heritage. Within this narrative, collectors were presented as the main actors, using their highly developed business skills to guide sales, manage dealers, and quickly build cultural institutions. With all the coverage of auction sales, *en bloc* buying, and record-breaking prices, American readers were intrigued both by the inaccessibility of this rich man's hobby, and the potential accessibility of the books they collected – items intended ultimately to be gifted to the American public. More perceptive readers soon questioned the true accessibility of such public gifts, with one 1920 *Los Angeles Times* article labelling the Huntington Library both a 'Bastile [*sic*] of Books' and 'the Western Louvre of Learning'.[312]

It was readily accepted that art treasures required safeguarding appropriate to their material worth. For the reading public, the monetary value of art objects always remained central to the narrative of American collecting. When the Metropolitan Museum of Art was formally dedicated in 1880, the gathered trustees were reminded to approach collecting in terms of fiscal pragmatism:

> Think of it, ye millionaires of many markets, what glory
> may yet be yours, if you only listen to our advice, to convert
> pork into porcelain, grain and produce into priceless pot-
> tery, the rude ores of commerce into sculptured marble, and
> railroad shares and mining stocks – things which perish

---

[310] Ibid., 188; See also N. Harris, *Cultural Excursions: Marketing Appetites and Cultural Tastes in Modern America* (Chicago: University Chicago Press, 1990), p. 267.

[311] G. T. Tanselle, 'A Rationale of Collecting', *Studies in Bibliography*, 51 (1998), p. 25.

[312] 'Bastile [*sic*] of Books Now Nearing Completion', *Los Angeles Times*, 25 March 1920, Part II, p. 1.

without using, and which in the next financial panic shall
surely shrivel like parched scrolls.[313]

The most successful dealers – both British and American – not only satisfied
their customer's material desires but convinced them that the books they
acquired were sound investments, destined to be permanently valuable. If
the major private libraries functioned as sites of national identity, they also
served as narrative-producing institutions, and this was largely a result of
transatlantic commercial efforts. Dealers leaked (sometimes embellished)
sales' figures to national news organisations, ensuring that the public was
made aware of enormous sums being spent. For private collectors, dealers
and auctioneers strove to make the acquisition of rare books a particularly
glamorous affair. Even catalogues were increasingly orientated away from
members of the trade and towards the private collector, with entries made
more detailed, authoritative, and attractive. Together, these elements
helped contribute to record-breaking auction sales. Bidding at auction
was, in reality, 'a game for professionals, not amateurs', and private
collectors were liable to 'throw [money] about in the auction room as
they would never do in a bookshop'.[314] Some dealers, like George
D. Smith, even impacted how other dealers bid during auctions, forcing
them to pay higher prices than they might have originally intended. Ever-
increasing prices became closely associated with the rare book market. As
a result, the drama of the auction room became a source of public fascination, advertising the skills of book-brokers and the dramas of intense
consumer desire, against the backdrop of an expectation that immense
personal wealth would benefit America.

The glittering surface of book buying could be effective, and lucrative,
but it required intensive efforts by dealers. Books travelled back and forth
across the Atlantic, and from dealer to dealer, sometimes without being sold
for considerable stretches of time. Nonetheless, book-brokers had to promote their stock to clients, emphasizing the desirability, provenance, and
rarity of high-priced items. The realities of the trade were frequently

---

[313] C. Tomkins, *Merchants and Masterpieces* (New York: E. P. Dutton, 1970), p. 23.
[314] Ibid., 128, 130.

concealed beneath industry myth, painstakingly-forged personal relation-ships, and carefully constructed catalogues. One particularly convenient rumour that circulated was about dealers being selective – at times reluc-tant – sellers, of only releasing certain books to certain collectors; while in some cases this may have been true, the myth of selective commercialism also served to foster important relationships between dealers and buyers. More specifically, it gave the buyer a great deal of agency, suggesting that their collecting agenda had earned commercial sanction. It also elevated the collector's role in terms of nurturing bibliographical discovery. However, if members of the commercial network helped cultivate such assumptions, they also challenged them. Carter noted that bibliographical findings are made possible through a well-functioning commercial book market, not simply the efforts of individual collectors.[315] Graham Pollard went even further, suggesting that only a bookseller had access to a wide enough range of books to address some of the thornier bibliographical questions.[316]

No commercial myth, however, has been as impactful for American collectors as that suggesting that England was being stripped of all its textual treasures in the years 1890 to 1929. Purchases of important English rare books by American collectors attracted considerable public comment – varying from praise to condemnation on both sides of the Atlantic. What received far less attention in the public press was the degree to which this myth at times benefited transatlantic dealers and British sellers. Opportunities for commercial profit were in fact potentially enhanced by public outcry over the American acquisition of British national treasures. As one contemporary commentator explained:

> When an item of great rarity and great value is sought by an institution, it is usual to raise a special fund by public subscrip-tion or through an appeal to some philanthropic individual. The results are most satisfactory when this can be done secretly; for once public attention is drawn to such an undertaking, the value

---

[315] Carter, 'Bibliography', pp. 222–3.

[316] D. McKitterick, 'Books, Libraries, and Society: The Past Ever with Us', *Libraries & Culture*, 27(3) (1992), p. 239.

of the object, whether it be of great antiquity or almost of to-day, is woefully exaggerated.[317]

American collectors pursuing national treasures were understandably incentivised to justify their need to collect such items. Some chose to publicise lofty collecting ideals, some drew public attention to the lavish conditions in which such items would be housed, and some emphasised the difficulty of capturing such treasures at all. In many cases, transatlantic attention only accelerated the collecting and solidified what may have once been tenuous collecting agendas. Altogether this gave the impression that, as well as being sites of national identity and narrative-producing institutions, private American libraries were highly contested spaces. The reality, however, was more complex.

Significantly, beneath the public outcry rested the efforts of dealers, curators, and British sellers who made such sales possible at all. One observer described the conditions on Bond Street just prior to the outbreak of the war:

> A long series of phenomenally successful seasons had brought great prosperity to the dealers, money was plentiful, and anxiety to obtain fine things, regardless of price, had never been keener. Galleries and shelves were well packed with valuable stock, and the autumnal invasion of American collectors and dealers was looked forward to with every anticipation of good business.[318]

Both before and following the war, British dealers actively pursued and maintained lucrative relationships with those same Americans publicly accused of stripping England of its national heritage. By 1914 Sabin supplied Rosenbach with enough stock for Rosenbach's biographers to refer to him as 'Sabin's best customer', and by 1919 many of Quaritch's customers, whether dealers or collectors, were American.[319] These could be

---

[317] Currie, *Fishers*, p. 194.

[318] W. Roberts, 'Art and Book Sales during and after the War', *The National Review*, 74 (1919), p. 375.

[319] Wolf and Fleming, *Rosenbach*, p. 86; A. Freeman and J. I. Freeman, *Anatomy of an Auction: Rare Books at Ruxley Lodge* (London: Book Collector, 1990), p. 101.

discriminating buyers, with one English contemporary noting that the wealthy American buyer 'is not such a fool as many English people – with things to sell – sometimes think. He does not mind paying a big price for a fine article, but he does not often pay an absurd sum for an inferior one'.[320] Americans were indeed buying remarkable articles from England, and for good reason. American demand for rare books was met with a transatlantic commercial network poised to ensure that such collectors were not often disappointed. At the same time, the trade in rare books represented more than an exchange of goods and money in both Britain and America. The narratives constructed around these exchanges represent a crucial element in the history of these precious objects, demonstrating the ways in which those involved in the book trade have helped to shape ideas about pre-modern books.

[320] Roberts, 'Art and Book Sales', p. 381.

Abbreviations

NACF	The National Art-Collections Fund
NYT	*The New York Times*
PW	*The Publishers' Weekly*

Select Bibliography

Adams Jr., F. B. (1964). *An Introduction to the Pierpont Morgan Library*, New York: Pierpont Morgan Library.

Allen, F. L. (1931). *Only Yesterday*, New York: Blue Ribbon.

Allen, F. L. (1949). *The Great Pierpont Morgan*, New York: Harper & Brothers.

Allen, F. L. (1952). *The Big Change, America Transforms Itself 1900–1915*, New York: Harper & Brothers.

Ardizzone, H. (2007). *An Illuminated Life: Belle da Costa Greene's Journey from Prejudice to Privilege*, New York: W. W. Norton.

Auchincloss, L. (1990). *J. P. Morgan: The Financier as Collector*, New York: Harry N. Abrams.

Basbanes, N. A. (1995). *A Gentle Madness: Bibliophiles, Bibliomaniacs, and the Eternal Passion for Books*, New York: Henry Holt.

Basbanes, N. A. (2001). *Patience and Fortitude*, New York: Harper Collins.

Behrman, S. N. (1952). *Duveen*, New York: Random House.

Bennett, J. Q. (1967). Portman Square to New Bond Street, or How to Make Money Though Rich. *The Book Collector*, 16(3), 323–39.

Bliss, L. E. (1939). The Research Facilities of the Huntington Library. *Huntington Library Quarterly*, 32, 131–5.

Braesel, M. (2019). *William Morris und die Buchmalerie*, Cologne: Böhlau.

Brown, M. P. (2006). *The Luttrell Psalter: A Facsimile*, London: British Library.

Bruccoli, M. (1986). *The Fortunes of Mitchell Kennerley, Bookman*, New York: Harcourt Brace Jovanovich.

Burgess, G. (1912). The Battle of the Books. *Collier's Magazine*, 10 February, 17.

Canfield, C. (1974). *The Incredible Pierpont Morgan: Financier and Art Collector*, New York: Harper & Row.

Cannon, C. (1941). *American Book Collectors and Collecting from Colonial Times to the Present*, New York: H. W. Wilson.

Carlton, W. N. C. (1927). Henry Edwards Huntington. *American Collector*, 4, 165–7.

Carter, J. (1948). *Taste and Technique in Book-Collecting: A Study of Recent Developments in Great Britain and the United States*, Cambridge: Cambridge University Press.

Carter, J. (1954). Bibliography and the Rare Book Trade. *The Papers of the Bibliographical Society of America*, 48(3), 219–29.

Cleaver, L. (2017). The Western Manuscript Collection of Alfred Chester Beatty (ca. 1915–1930). *Manuscript Studies*, 2(2), 445–82.

Cleaver, L. (2020). Charles William Dyson Perrins as a Collector of Medieval and Renaissance Manuscripts c. 1900–1920. *Perspectives médiévales*, 41.

Cole, G. W. (1915). Book Collectors as Benefactors of Public Libraries. *The Papers of the Bibliographical Society of America*, 3, 47–110.

Cole, G. W. (1920a). *Bibliography – A Forecast*, Chicago: University of Chicago Press.

Cole, G. W. (1920b). The Henry E. Huntington Library. In *Annual Publication of the Historical Society of Southern California*, Los Angeles: Historical Society of Southern California, pp. 24–9.

Cole, G. W. (1922). The Huntington Library. *Library Journal*, 47, 745–50.

Cole, G. W. (1923). *The Henry E. Huntington Library and Art Gallery*, New York: R. R. Bowker.

Currie, B. W. (1931). *Fishers of Books*, Boston: Little, Brown.

Davison, P., ed. (1998). *The Book Encompassed: Studies in Twentieth-Century Bibliography*, New Castle: Oak Knoll Press.

de Hamel, C. (2006). Cockerell as Entrepreneur. *The Book Collector*, 55(1), 49–72.

De Ricci, S. (1960). *English Collectors of Books and Manuscripts*, Bloomington: Indiana University Press reprint.

Dickinson, D. C. (1986). *Dictionary of American Book Collectors*, New York: Greenwood Press.

Dickinson, D. C. (1988). Mr. Huntington and Mr. Smith. *The Book Collector*, 37(3), 367–94.

Dickinson, D. C. (1995). *Henry E. Huntington's Library of Libraries*, San Marino: Huntington Library Press.

Dickinson, D. C. (1998). *Dictionary of American Antiquarian Bookdealers*, Westport: Greenwood Press.

Douglas, A. (1996). *Terrible Honesty: Mongrel Manhattan in the 1920s*, New York: Noonday Press.

Duveen, J. H. (1938). *Secrets of an Art Dealer*, New York: Dutton.

Duveen, J. H. (1957). *The Rise of the House of Duveen*, New York: Knopf.

Emerson, R. W. (1856). *English Traits and Representative Men*, Boston: Phillips, Samson.

Folger, H. C. (1907). A Unique First Folio. *The Outlook*, 87(12), 687–91.

Freeman, A., & Freeman, J. I. (1990). *Anatomy of an Auction: Rare Books at Ruxley Lodge, 1919*, London: Smith Settle.

Granniss, R. (1939). American Book Collecting and the Growth of Libraries. In H. Lehmann-Haupt, ed., *The Book in America: A History of the Making, the Selling, and the Collecting of Books in the United States*, New York: R. R. Bowker, pp. 295–375.

Gwara, S. (2020a). Je me souviens: The Forgotten Collection of Medieval and Renaissance Manuscripts Owned by Gerald E. Hart of Montreal. In H. Anderson & D. T. Gura, eds., *Between the Text and the Page: Studies on the Transmission of Medieval Ideas in Honour of Frank T. Coulson*, Toronto: Pontifical Institute of Mediaeval Studies, pp. 255–88.

Gwara, S. (2020b). Peddling Wonderment, Selling Privilege: Launching the Market for Medieval Books in Antebellum New York. *Perspectives médiévales*, 41.

Hale, G. E. (1927). The Huntington Library and Art Gallery. *Scribner's Magazine*, 82(1), 31–43.

Harris, N. (1983). The Gilded Age Reconsidered Once Again. *Archives of American Art Journal*, 23(4), 9–18.

Harris, N. (1990). *Cultural Excursions: Marketing Appetites and Cultural Tastes in Modern America*, Chicago: University of Chicago Press.

Hawthorne, N. (1863). *Our Old Home: A Series of English Sketches*, Columbus: Ohio State University Press.

Heartman, C. F. (1938). *Twenty-Five Years in the Auction Business, and What Now?*, privately printed.

Hellman, G. S. (1927). *Lanes of Memory*, New York: Alfred A. Knopf.

Herrmann, F. (1980). *Sotheby's: Portrait of an Auction House*, London: Chatto & Windus.

Hopkin, F. M. (1922). The Golden Age of Book Collecting: An Interview with Dr. Rosenbach. *The Publishers' Weekly*, 28 October, 1541–3.

Hovey, C. (1912). *The Life Story of J. Pierpont Morgan: A Biography*, New York: Sturgis & Walton.

Ives, B. (1891). *Catalogue of the Collection of Books and Manuscripts Belonging to Mr. Brayton Ives of New-York*, New York: De Vinne Press.

Jackson, W. A. (1949). America. In *The Bibliographical Society, 1892–1942: Studies in Retrospect*, Cambridge: Cambridge University Press, pp. 185–8.

James, H. (1905). *English Hours*, Boston: Houghton, Mifflin.

James, H. (1907). *The American Scene*, New York: Harper & Brothers.

James, H. (1911). *The Outcry*, New York: Charles Scribner's Sons.

James, M. R. (1906). *Catalogue of Manuscripts and Early Printed Books from the Libraries of William Morris, Richard Bennett, Bertram Fourth Earl of Ashburnham, and Other Sources Now Forming Portion of the Library of J. Pierpont Morgan*, London: Chiswick Press.

Johnson, M. E. (1932). The Henry E. Huntington Library. *The English Journal*, 21(7), 529–33.

Joline, A. H. (1902). *Meditations of an Autograph Hunter*, New York: Harper & Brothers.

Keppler, U. J. (1911). The Magnet. *Puck*, 21 June.

King, F. A. (1913). The Complete Collector. *The Bookman*, 36(1), 510–23.

Korey, M. E., & Mortimer, R. (1990). Fifteen Women Book Collectors. *Gazette of the Grolier Club*, 42, 49–87.

Lang, A. (1913). *Books and Bookmen*, London: Longmans, Green.

Leach, W. (1993). *Land of Desire: Merchants, Power and the Rise of a New American Culture*, New York: Pantheon.

Lears, J. T. J. (1981). *No Place of Grace: Antimodernism and the Transformation of American Culture, 1880–1920*, Chicago: University of Chicago Press.

Lehmann-Haupt, H. (1939). *The Book in America: A History of the Making, Selling, and the Collecting of Books in the United States*, New York: R. R. Bowker.

Linenthal, R. A. (2007). 'The Collectors are Far More Particular Than You Think:' Selling Manuscripts to America. *Manuscripta*, 51(1), 131–42.

Livingston, L. S. (1914). An Appreciation. In *A Sentimental Library: Comprising Books Formerly Owned by Famous Writers, Presentation Copies, Manuscripts, and Drawings Collected and Described by Harry B. Smith*, New York: De Vinne Press, pp. xvii–xxvi.

Lockwood, A. (1981). *Passionate Pilgrims: The American Traveler in Great Britain, 1800–1914*, New York: Cornwall Books.

Lynd, J. N. (1912). The Bloodless Battles for Books of the Bibliophiles. *The New York Herald*, 14 January.

Lynes, R. (1949). *The Tastemakers*, New York: Harper & Brothers.

Mandelbrote, G., ed. (2006). *Out of Print & Into Profit: A History of the Rare and Secondhand Book Trade in Britain in the Twentieth Century*, London: British Library.

Mandler, P. (1997). *The Fall and Rise of the Stately Home*, New Haven: Yale University Press.

McKay, G. L. (1937). *American Book Auction Catalogues, 1713–1934*, New York: New York Public Library.

McKitterick, D. (1992). Books, Libraries, and Society: The Past Ever with Us. *Libraries & Culture*, 27(3), 231–51.

McKitterick, D., ed. (2009). *The Cambridge History of the Book in Britain, Volume VI: 1830–1914*, Cambridge: Cambridge University Press.

Mencken, H. L. (1937). *The American Language*, New York: Alfred A. Knopf.

Morris, L. A. (1988). *Rosenbach Abroad*, Philadelphia: Rosenbach Museum and Library.

Morris, L. A. (1997). Bernard Alfred Quaritch in America. *The Book Collector*, special number for the 150th Anniversary of Bernard Quaritch, 118–33.

Munby, A. N. L. (1960). *The Dispersal of the Phillipps Library*, Phillipps Studies 5, Cambridge: Cambridge University Press.

Munby, A. N. L., & Turner, L. W. (1969). *The Flow of Books and Manuscripts*, Los Angeles: William Andrews Clark Memorial Library.

Myers, R., & Harris, M., eds. (1996). *Antiquaries, Book Collectors and the Circles of Learning*, Winchester: Oak Knoll Press.

Myers, R., Harris, M., & Mandelbrote, G., eds. (2001). *Under the Hammer: Book Auctions since the Seventeenth Century*, New Castle: Oak Knoll Press.

Needham, P., ed. (1976). *William Morris and the Art of the Book*, Oxford: Oxford University Press.

Newton, A. E. (1918). *The Amenities of Book Collecting*, Boston: Atlantic Monthly Press.

Otness, H. M. (1988). A Room Full of Books: The Life and Slow Death of the American Residential Library. *Libraries & Culture*, 23(2), 111–34.

Panayotova, S. (2010). Cockerell and Riches. In J. H. Marrow, R. A. Linenthal, & W. Noel, eds., *The Medieval Book: Glosses from Friends & Colleagues of Christopher de Hamel*, 't Goy-Houten: Hes & De Graaf, pp. 377–86.

Partridge, B. (1922). Autolycus U.S.A. *Punch*, 24 May.

Pettegree, A., & Weduwen, A. D. (2021). *The Library: A Fragile History*, London: Profile Books.

Purcell, M. (2017). *The Country House Library*, New Haven: Yale University Press.

Quaritch, B. (1890). *Exhibition of Books & MSS by Bernard Quaritch of London*, London: Quaritch.

Roberts, W. (1910). A King of Manuscript Collectors. *The National Review*, 55, 646–52.

Roberts, W. (1919). Art and Book Sales during and after the War. *The National Review*, 74, 375–87.

Rosenbach, A. S. W. (1927a). *Books and Bidders: The Adventures of a Bibliophile*, Boston: Little, Brown.

Rosenbach, A. S. W. (1927b). Why America Buys England's Books. *The Atlantic Monthly*, 140(4), 452–9.

Rosenbach, A. S. W. (1931). *Henry C. Folger as a Collector*, New Haven: privately printed.

Roth, L. H., ed. (1987). *J. Pierpont Morgan, Collector, European Decorative Arts from the Wadsworth Atheneum*, Wisbech: Balding and Mansell.

Rubin, J. S. (1992). *The Making of Middlebrow Culture*, Chapel Hill: University of North Carolina Press.

Ryskamp, C. (1984). Abbie Pope, Portrait of a Bibliophile. *The Book Collector*, 33(1), 39–53.

Saarinen, A. (1958). *The Proud Possessors: The Lives, Times, and Tastes of Some Adventurous American Art Collectors*, New York: Random House.

Saltzman, C. (2008). *Old Masters, New World: America's Raid on Europe's Great Pictures 1880-World War I*, New York: Viking Press.

Satterlee, H. L. (1939). *J. Pierpont Morgan: An Intimate Portrait*, New York: Macmillan.

Schad, R. O. (1931). Henry Edwards Huntington – The Founder and the Library. *The Huntington Library Bulletin*, 1, 3–32.

Schwarz, A. L. (2006). *Dear Mr. Cockerell, Dear Mr. Peirce: An Annotated Description of the Correspondence of Sydney C. Cockerell and Harold Peirce in the Grolier Club Archive*, High Wycombe: Rivendale Press.

Shaddy, R. A. (1994). A World of Sentimental Attachments: The Cult of Collecting, 1890–1930. *The Book Collector*, 43, 185–200.

Shorter, C. K. (1925a). A Literary Letter: The Ideal Bookman. *The Sphere*, 16 May, 202.

Shorter, C. K. (1925b). A Literary Letter: The Solidarity of Book-Collecting. *The Sphere*, 10 January, 38.

Smith, H. B. (1914). *A Sentimental Library: Comprising Books Formerly Owned by Famous Writers, Presentation Copies, Manuscripts, and Drawings Collected and Described by Harry B. Smith*, New York: De Vinne Press.

Sowerby, E. M. (1987). *Rare People and Rare Books*, Williamsburg: Bookpress.

Spender, S. (1975). *Love-Hate Relations: English and American Sensibilities*, New York: Vintage Books.

Stevens, M. (1973). The History of the *Towneley Plays*: Its History and Editions. *The Papers of the Bibliographical Society of America*, 67(3), 231–44.

Stoneman, W. P. (2007). 'Variously Employed': The Pre-Fitzwilliam Career of Sydney Carlyle Cockerell. *Transactions of the Cambridge Bibliographical Society*, 13(4), 345–62.

Strouse, J. (1999). *Morgan: American Financier*, New York: Random House.

Tanselle, G. T. (1998). A Rationale of Collecting. *Studies in Bibliography*, 51, 1–25.

Taylor, F. (1970). *Pierpont Morgan as Collector and Patron, 1837–1913*, New York: Pierpont Morgan Library.

Thompson, J. W. (1931). Wilfrid Michael Voynich. *Progress of Medieval Studies in the United States and Canada*, 90–2.

Thorpe, J. (1994). *Henry Edwards Huntington: A Biography*, Berkeley: University of California Press.

Tomkins, C. (1970). *Merchants and Masterpieces: The Story of the Metropolitan Museum of Art*, New York: E. P. Dutton.

Towner, W. (1970). *The Elegant Auctioneers*, New York: Hill and Wang.

Twycross, M. (2015). They Did Not Come Out of an Abbey in Lancashire: Francis Douce and the Manuscript of the Towneley Plays. *Medieval English Theatre*, 37, 149–65.

Witt, R. C. (1903). A Movement in Aid of Our National Art Collections. *Nineteenth Century and After*, 54, 651–9.

Wolf, E., & Fleming, J. F. (1960). *Rosenbach, a Biography*, Cleveland: World.

Wright, L. B. (1962). Huntington and Folger, Book Collectors with a Purpose. *The Atlantic Monthly*, 209, 70–4.

Wroth, L. C. (1949). *The First Quarter Century of the Pierpont Morgan Library: A Retrospective Exhibition in Honor of Belle Da Costa Green*, New York: Pierpont Morgan Library.

Acknowledgements

The research for this book has been undertaken as part of the CULTIVATE MSS project, which has received funding from the European Research Council (ERC) under the European Union's Horizon 2020 research and innovation programme (grant agreement no. 817988). The authors are very grateful to the staff at Bernard Quaritch Ltd., the British Library, the Bodleian Library, the Grolier Club, the Morgan Library, The Rosenbach Museum and the John Rylands Library for their help in accessing archival materials. They also want to thank Olivia Baskerville, Federico Botana, Sarah Churchwell, Christopher de Hamel, Ana de Oliveira Dias, Tony Edwards, Natalia Fantetti, Hannah Morcos, Pierre-Louis Pinault, Angéline Rais, William P. Stoneman, and René Zandbergen for discussion of ideas presented here, Spencer Ratcliff and the Denham family, and the peer-reviewers and the team at Cambridge University Press for their feedback.

Cambridge Elements ☰

Publishing and Book Culture

SERIES EDITOR
Samantha Rayner
University College London

Samantha Rayner is Professor of Publishing and Book Cultures at UCL. She is also Director of UCL's Centre for Publishing, co-Director of the Bloomsbury CHAPTER (Communication History, Authorship, Publishing, Textual Editing and Reading) and co-Chair of the Bookselling Research Network.

ASSOCIATE EDITOR
Leah Tether
University of Bristol

Leah Tether is Professor of Medieval Literature and Publishing at the University of Bristol. With an academic background in medieval French and English literature and a professional background in trade publishing, Leah has combined her expertise and developed an international research profile in book and publishing history from manuscript to digital.

ABOUT THE SERIES

This series aims to fill the demand for easily accessible, quality texts available for teaching and research in the diverse and dynamic fields of Publishing and Book Culture. Rigorously researched and peer-reviewed Elements will be published under themes, or 'Gatherings'. These Elements should be the first check point for researchers or students working on that area of publishing and book trade history and practice: we hope that, situated so logically at Cambridge University Press, where academic publishing in the UK began, it will develop to create an unrivalled space where these histories and practices can be investigated and preserved.

Cambridge Elements ≡

Publishing and Book Culture
Collecting the Book

Gathering Editor: Cynthia Johnston
Cynthia Johnston is a Lecturer in the History of the Book and
Communication at the Institute of English Studies, School of
Advanced Study, University of London where she directs the
MA programme in the History of the Book. Her research
interests focus on the history of book collecting and book
cultures.

ELEMENTS IN THE GATHERING

*The Trade in Rare Books and Manuscripts between Britain and America
c. 1890–1929*
Danielle Magnusson and Laura Cleaver

A full series listing is available at: www.cambridge.org/EPBC

Printed in the United States
by Baker & Taylor Publisher Services